A Dream,
A Goal,
Never a Reality

STANLEY RATLIFF

authorHOUSE®

AuthorHouse™
1663 Liberty Drive, Suite 200
Bloomington, IN 47403
www.authorhouse.com
Phone: 1-800-839-8640

First published by AuthorHouse 9/18/2008

ISBN: 978-1-4343-6622-1 (sc)

Printed in the United States of America
Bloomington, Indiana

This book is printed on acid-free paper.

Dedication

This book is dedicated to the memory of Calvin Ford, Christian Smith, Mrs. Joan Mc Duffy, my Aunt Dolly and my son Stanley Jr.

"I am the vine; you are the branches. If a man remains in me and I in him, he will bear much fruit; apart from me you can do nothing."

John 15:5 (New International Version)

Thank You

First and foremost I'd like to thank My Lord and Savior Jesus Christ for allowing me to write this book. I know that without Him this book would have never been completed. So thank you Jesus! You were right when you said "apart from you we can do nothing". I would like to thank Jonita Robinson for all the hard work of editing this book. Thank you, Jessie William for all of your pictures that you've saved and given me for this book. I'd like to thank my cousin Billy Avery for his support in giving me pictures and information that I wasn't clear on, and probably still not clear on. Thank you, Mrs. Cray for going through this book and correcting my bad grammar. I praise God for you. I'd like to thank Melvin for believing in me and putting the down payment on getting this book published. Thank you Ashley Pharis for all your help in communicating what I needed to Jonita and the publishing company. Thank you, Author House for your patience in working with me. Thank you to all of our family and friends who stood by Superior Movement's side and believed in us. Even though the dream never came to be, thank you all for the encouragement and support.

A very special thanks to my Pastor Wayne "Coach" Gordon and the Lawndale Community Church Family for believing in me and allowing me to use my talents and gifts for God's glory. Finally, I'd like to thank my wife Antoinette and sons Antonio, Antwane, and Andrew for allowing me time away from them to complete this book.

Table of Contents

Chapter 1	How It All Began	1
Chapter 2	The First Talent Show	6
Chapter 3	Getting It Together	10
Chapter 4	Our First Name	11
Chapter 5	The Coming of David	13
Chapter 6	The First Concert as Superior Movement	16
Chapter 7	First Concert at Farragut High	20
Chapter 8	Smitty As ManagerakaChristian Smith	25
Chapter 9	Summertime of '78	32
Chapter 10	Getting a Record Contract	38
Chapter 11	Shoot Outs During Concert	50
Chapter 12	Our Fan Club	53
Chapter 13	Our Equipment Got Stolen	56
Chapter 14	More Shows	59
Chapter 15	Trouble with the Record Company	63
Chapter 16	Calvin Goes to the Army	68
Chapter 17	Tyrone Goes to California	71
Chapter 18	Signing with L.P.M.	73
Chapter 19	Looking for a Deal	75
Chapter 20	Budweiser Showdown	78
Chapter 21	The Night of the Budweiser Showdown	80
Chapter 22	Second Time Around for a Record Deal	83
Chapter 23	The Jenita Contrell Story (Deal with Motown)	84
Chapter 24	Motown Sends a Telegram	92
Chapter 25	After the Storm	96
Chapter 26	Greg Becomes an Official Member	98
Chapter 27	Things Begin to Slow Down	99

CHAPTER 1

How It All Began

It all started back in Farragut High School in 1974. Five guys from the male chorus decided that they wanted to be in the school's upcoming talent show. It seemed so long ago that I don't really know how I ever became a part of these five guys.

Well anyway, there was Calvin Ford, William Unger, Tyrone Powell, Michael Avery, and myself, Stanley Ratliff. We began practicing down in the basement of Michael's brother. Every day after school we would rehearse. Oftentimes it was difficult to get things started, because some of the guys didn't feel that rehearsal was important. They figured that they could just go on stage and sound like angels. For example, William was always missing rehearsal. He was the "too cool" type.

Curls weren't in style back then, and thank God for that. William had a head full of hair, and it was in a style that they called an "afro." The afro look was the style back then, and everybody who had a lot of hair wore an afro. At first William was an okay person and we all got along very well because we came from the same grammar school. Then, all of a sudden, William's personality began to change. I'll tell you more about William later.

We (us five guys) were getting ready for the talent show, and the news spread around the school and neighborhood. People would come up to us and say, "I heard you guys are going to be in the talent show.

Good luck!" Some would just belch out a laugh and say, "Ooh, I can't wait!" Since everybody knew about us being in the talent show, we became small-time celebrities around the school and neighborhood. Girls started speaking to us more, and we loved it! They even started coming around our rehearsal place!

William would always be late for rehearsals, and he started to chase skirts and walk different—you know, all cool with a limp. If I remember correctly, I think he even had a cane occasionally. Let me stop talking about William.

Let's talk about Calvin. Calvin was a unique person in his own way. He was what some would call a chip off the old block. Calvin and I were on the football and basketball team at Farragut High School, so this gives me the right to talk about him, bless his soul. Anyway, Calvin was another person that was hard to get to rehearsal. He was a sports fanatic. Although he didn't always play well, he did know the rules forward and backward. When Calvin didn't show up for rehearsals, I knew where I could find him. I knew that if he wasn't at Marcy Center playing baseball, he would be at the Better Boys Foundation trying to play basketball. If he wasn't there, then I knew

MARCY CENTER 15*TH* & SPRINGFIED
This is where we played ball and did outside concerts

he was over at some girl's house. He had about four or five girlfriends, and I knew where each one lived. So believe me, when I wanted to find Calvin, I did. I did the same thing for football practice. We had football practice in the mornings and afternoons, and I would make sure Calvin was with me when I went.

Calvin had a really good voice. It was a nice falsetto when he stayed on pitch. This was his only fault when he sung. The boy couldn't stay on pitch for anything in the world! At times we would be harmonizing and somebody would be off pitch. Normally we would keep singing and the person that was off pitch would jump back on pitch, but not Calvin. He would be in a world of his own. Someone would have to shout to let him know he was off pitch. Finally everyone would laugh, and we would show him what part he should be singing.

Next there was Michael. Michael is my cousin, and he was the best singer out of all of us. This I must say ... he had a damn good voice! He could sing anything from Bing Crosby's "I'm Dreaming of a White Christmas" to Al Green's "Love and Happiness." The guy was awesome. Anyway, he was the lead singer of the group. We did whatever he said, because if we didn't, he wouldn't sing. In addition to our group, Michael had sung in his own band for years. He had much more experience than we did. If I can recall, I think Michael missed of lot of rehearsals also. As a matter of fact, I'm sure he did. Nevertheless, we did get things together before the talent show.

Did I forget anyone? Oh! Of course, Tyrone and me. Well, I put us last because we were sort of in the background. The other guys had better voices, and they were more outspoken than we were. We were just glad to be part of it all. It was a good feeling to have people come up to us and ask us if we were singing in the talent show. Okay, Tyrone ... Tyrone is my buddy, but since I'm writing the book, I might as well tell it all. Tyrone was on the basketball team at Farragut High School. He played varsity and Calvin and I played on the sophomore team together. Tyrone loved to chase girls too, but he didn't let it interfere with what he wanted to do. He often had trouble finding his note. If he couldn't hold a note, he wasn't ashamed to say he didn't know his part. He would ask for help, and we would

3

help him, unlike Calvin, who just kept on singing like nothing was wrong.

Tyrone used to miss a lot of classes back then. He would only attend the male chorus class and drama class. Try to get him to come to English class and he would say, "No way!" Tyrone wouldn't go to class for anything in the world! He would just hang out all day around the music area from 9:00 to 4:00. The girlfriends he had were real cutie-pies. Sometimes I would ask myself, "How *does* he do it?" I mean he had some beautiful ladies! Some were even older than he was. Tyrone had sheer determination, and that's why he stayed in the group.

Now, did we cover everybody? We didn't? Oh, how could I forget? Me! Well, there isn't too much to say about me. I was the innocent one. It's the truth! I was the all-American shy boy. I was in a lot of organizations while in high school. I was on the football and basketball teams, the drama club, and the male chorus and was president of the National Honor Society. Sounds good, doesn't it? But there was something missing … a girlfriend. Everyone had one but me. I was too busy to even spend time with one. Besides, I had to be in the house no later than 9:00 p.m. By that time, we were finished with rehearsal, and it was time for me to go home. That's when all the guys and girls got together. So every day after rehearsal, the guys would talk about what happened the night before while I was in the house. Some guys had all the luck.

Now don't get me wrong, I did have friends, and most of them *were* girls! Lots of times I would dream of going out with them. However, I didn't want a good relationship to end if I were to approach one of them the wrong way. Every now and then I would end up with a girlfriend, but most of the time I was occupied with school and rehearsal.

Now that I've covered everyone, let's get back to the talent show. Time was running out, and the show must go on. It was the day before the show, and we all had gone down to Maxwell Street and bought our pants. Maxwell Street was a place where you could go and bargain with the owner. Since Tyrone worked at a department store, he was supposed to pick up the shirts for us. Besides, he was the only one in the group who had a job and a car. So before rehearsal, we were waiting for Tyrone to bring the shirts, and finally he showed up. Do you know what he brought back? He brought back five *loud*, pink, ruffled shirts! You know the kind Tom Jones use to wear? Nevertheless we had to accept it, because time was running out. We began rehearsing for the last time, and everything seemed to be all right.

NOBLE SQUARE DAYTON, OHIO
Left to right: Calvin, David, Billy, Tyrone, Stanley

CHAPTER 2

The First Talent Show

"Okay ladies and gentlemen," the M.C. said and began introducing us. There we were back stage, nervous with butterflies in our stomachs. The band began playing, and we came out. The audience was going wild! Girls were screaming, and it was great! We were singing "Miracle" by the Stylistics. We sounded just like the record. Everything went perfect. After the show, we went to our rehearsal place and celebrated. We started to think, "Why not get serious?" We decided to keep practicing and do the next talent show. So when we got back to school the next Monday, everybody was congratulating us. I've never had so many compliments in my life, especially from girls! We all loved it! Compliments went on for about a week. You think it was hard getting guys to rehearsal for the first talent show? The second talent show was worse! Everybody seemingly got a big head, William especially. This guy wanted to do all the lead singing, and so did my cousin Michael. So there was a conflict there. Calvin was still the same Calvin. He was still at the basketball court or playing baseball or at one of his so called girlfriends' houses. Rehearsal was just awful. We rehearsed off and on, but not as much as we did for the first talent show.

Here it was, the day of the show. This time we wore the same thing, except we added a bow tie to the pink Tom Jones-looking shirts. The bow tie was enormous! You know the kind that was too big for the collar ... Mickey Mouse? That's it! Mickey Mouse wore one all the time. Anyway, here it was showtime once again. The band began playing, the girls screaming, and of course the butterflies were free (a football saying). We were now on stage, and Michael went to grab his microphone. He began singing. The rest of us hadn't started to sing yet because we were the background vocalists. We could hear that the band was playing one thing and Michael was singing another thing. We got confused. We didn't know if we should come in and sing along with Michael or the band. We had to make a decision and quick. So we did, and we sang along with Michael. It sounded terrible. I knew that if it sounded bad to us, that it had to sound bad to the audience. I was hoping that if the girls screamed loud enough then maybe, just maybe, they wouldn't hear us very well.

Left to right: Stanley, Calvin, Billy, David, and Tyrone

Nevertheless, we were singing and the band was playing. You would think that at some point we would catch up with the band. But no way! We were lost through the whole song. Michael finally walked off the stage, leaving us there. The rest of us were waiting for someone to follow Michael off stage. It took a couple of minutes and the next person left and the rest of us just followed. There we were, arguing backstage, blaming it on each other. Michael said

7

we messed up, and we said Michael messed up. So later on in the show, we had a second chance to make up for our mistake. Only this time Michael refused to go back on stage. Also, I was going to do the lead on the next song. Me! I never sang lead in my life! When I think back, I couldn't sing anyway. Mr. Gans, our chorus director, came backstage and persuaded Michael and the rest of the group to go back on and do the other song. So here we went again. When we went out there, I grabbed my microphone and started to sing. Some of the audience was laughing, and others were listening. We even had our friends laughing at us. One guy I remember so well is a guy by the name of Baby Bass. This guy weighed at least three hundred pounds. Where on earth did he get the name Baby Bass? Anyway, Baby would always, and I mean always, come to our shows just to laugh. This particular show he was sitting right in the front row. You couldn't miss him! He was just laughing away. As I was singing, I couldn't help but see him pointing, laughing, and holding his stomach. Did I sound *that* bad? This guy was having the time of his life! Finally we got off stage. We might as well have stayed off stage, because the second time was no better than the first time. This time after the show, we didn't celebrate. We were all too mad at each other. Everybody was blaming it on one another. The next Monday at school, Mr. Gans explained to us whose fault it was, and he said that it was Michael's fault. He said that Michael had come in too soon. Now Michael found this hard to believe because he was the one with the most experience. He was not supposed to mess up. Mr. Gans said not to worry about it, and he told us to keep practicing and we would do better the next time. There was never a next time for the five of us. First, William got big-headed and never came to rehearsal. He had gotten too cool and left the group. So that left Michael, Calvin, Tyrone, and I.

Michael's brother, Billy, was home from college. He was attending Illinois State University. He could sing just as well as Michael, so we asked him to join us. Billy wasn't really into singing, but I guess he said, "What the hell?" Most of the time Tyrone and I would be the first ones at rehearsal. Then within an hour or so, everybody else showed up. Since we were just starting out as a group, we didn't have any equipment. All we had was the record player. We would gather around it and sing. First someone would put a record on, and then we would ask each other if everyone had their part. If we all said yes, then we would take the needle off and start singing a cappella. We sang a cappella a lot in the male chorus at school. Then we would take a break, and someone used to always bring something to drink. Most of the time it was a six-pack and a fifth of shake and bake. Oh yes, shake and bake was the thing back then! Shake and bake was a fifth of white port and a package of lemon Kool-Aid. You pour the Kool-Aid in the bottle and then you shake it. By the end of rehearsal, everybody was toasted. Thank God that those days of shake and bake are over. We were so young; we really didn't know any better.

CHAPTER 3

Getting It Together

So here we went again ... Michael, Tyrone, Calvin, Billy, and me. We were preparing for a talent show at Jones Commercial High School. Getting ready for this show was just as hard as the talent shows before. Michael missed a lot of rehearsals and so did Calvin. But we got it together, and the show was okay. We passed and that was it. We decided that we wanted to keep doing the talent shows, so off and on we would rehearse. We could see that Michael wasn't too interested in singing with us anymore. He would come to rehearsal any time he wanted to. No one would say anything because we didn't want him to leave. This went on for several weeks. Finally his brother Billy spoke up. He was fed up with Michael missing rehearsal. He told Michael how we all felt about the situation. Michael then told us how he felt. He said he wanted to go back to being a solo singer. So he quit. Oh man! Now what? Tyrone, Calvin, Billy, and I thought about it and vowed to keep this thing going. We had gotten even more serious.

CHAPTER 4

Our First Name

Well, here we were again and wouldn't you believe it—another talent show was coming up. This time we were prepared. We adopted our very first name. We called ourselves the Fourth Movement. We rehearsed, rehearsed, and rehearsed some more. We even started to do dance routines while rehearsing. Tyrone was the best dancer, so he made up most of the steps. Although Calvin and I danced like stiff zombies, we kept in step. We placed pop bottles in front of us and pretended they were microphone stands. Showtime was getting nearer. We were getting better, and everything was falling into place. We were getting ready for our last rehearsal with a real band. The band that was to play for us had its own vocalists. They were called the Copastatics. We were feeling a little nervous because we were in their rehearsal space and the Copastatics' vocalists were there staring at us. If you were there, you could have felt the vibes. After we had finished rehearsing, the band congratulated us. They said we were ready!

Once again it was showtime. We were back stage. We had on black pants, black shoes, black vests, and those darn pink ruffled shirts. We also had on the Mickey Mouse bow ties. But we did look different, because we didn't wear the same exact uniforms.

The band began playing. Here we went again. Everybody in Farragut's auditorium was screaming. We came out, and guess

11

who the first person we saw in the audience was? You guessed it! Baby Bass, three hundred pounds and all! He was laughing, but we fooled him this time. We got down! We sang "Superstar" by the Temptations and "Can't Seem to Forget You" by Heaven and Earth (a local group). It was great! After the show, we celebrated in Billy's brother's basement. We had our shake and bake and a six-pack. We talked and laughed about the show. We talked about who missed a step and who went off pitch at times. But nothing was major.

CHAPTER 5

The Coming of David

At the next rehearsal, we talked about our harmony. We didn't think that it was strong enough. Something was missing. So we decided to look for a fifth member. We didn't waste any time auditioning people. We auditioned about five guys from the male chorus, but none of them worked out. Then one day we sat down and talked about asking the new kid who had just joined the chorus. I said no because I didn't think he would work out. For God's sake, he was a freshman! I was outvoted, so we tried the kid. At first I said, "No way." He was holding back. He was too quiet, but then once he got used to us, he was just like one of the fellas. So here he was, Mr. David William. He was now one of us. However, now we couldn't shut him up! At first he was so quiet and shy. Now he always had something to say. We didn't have to watch the news on television because David knew everybody's business around us and wasn't ashamed to tell us.

We all talked and rehearsed. We decided that we wanted this to be our career. We became really dedicated, and were determined to make this work. We then started to put our own band together. This wasn't hard because there was a band that rehearsed right across the street from the grammar school we used to attend. We asked them if they would play behind us, and they accepted the invitation. I knew two of the guys in the band very well. Their names were Roosevelt Hayes and Wayne Hill. I knew them from way back when we played

13

in the grammar school band together. I used to play saxophone and Wayne and Roosevelt played clarinet. The other guy that played in this band was Wayne's brother, who played drums. Wayne played keyboards and Roosevelt played lead guitar. Roosevelt left for college and was then replaced by another friend of ours by the name of Johnnie Hubbard.

So now it's about November 1976. We were more serious than ever. We began looking for a manager. There was a friend of ours from the male chorus who was already in a group named Michael Moore. He was in a group with his friend and two nieces. The name of their group was North, South, East, and West. They were much younger than us. They had a record out and were performing all over the Midwest area. So we went to talk to his parents, who also managed them, and we asked them if they would consider managing us. They never did give us a direct answer. They just told us that we could rehearse in their basement and they would let their kids listen to us.

We used to go down in their basement every day and rehearse. Calvin couldn't stand going over there. The reason he didn't like it was because they had told us to get rid of him. Remember, I had to always find Calvin to rehearse, and they noticed that. However, we didn't want to drop him from the group. Not yet, because we were determined to make it work. I'll admit that Calvin was messing up, but because he was our friend, we decided to keep him. We kept rehearsing for about five months in the Moores' basement and do you believe that they hardly even listened to us? Most of the time we would come over there and they would tell us to go downstairs and shut the door. I think that out of the five months we were down there, they only listened to us about four times! We grew tired of this and asked them what was up. We needed to know. They said Mr. Moore was interested in managing us. So we practiced a little longer. Then Mr. Moore got sick. About a month later Mr. Moore died, and we headed back to Michael's brother's basement.

Well, here we were again, back in Michael's brother's basement. By the way, Michael's brother's name is Junior. Junior was the oldest of the Avery brothers and wasn't into singing at all. We were glad that he allowed us to rehearse in his place. So we practiced with the three-piece band that we had. The band members were just starting out too, so you can imagine how it must have sounded. Eight bodies down in a little old basement! We didn't have any microphones, so we really couldn't hear how we sounded when the band played. We practiced for a while but never played together at a show. I'll tell you why. You won't believe it!

One sunny weekend, my cousin Carl, Michael Avery, and I were drinking shake and bake. We had gotten pretty bubbly. All of a sudden, Carl decided he wanted to play the drums. The band had left their drum set in the basement for the weekend. Carl got overly excited. He was banging, banging, and banging. I'm sure everyone in the neighborhood heard him. Then Michael joined him. They took turns on who could beat the drums the loudest. Then Michael hit a hole in the snare drum. They thought it was funny. Then Carl laid the bass drum down flat and stepped into it! They loved it! I was just sitting there looking, and I felt sorry for Wayne's brother (the drummer). Now he didn't have any drums to play! When the band found out what had happened, they didn't come around anymore. We began rehearsing among ourselves once again. There was no more band. We had to find one really fast, because there was a show coming up. This time it was a real show, not a talent show! There was this guy named David Glover we knew. He played in the band at Farragut. We asked him if he knew a band, and he said yes. As a matter of fact, he was in the band himself. We had set up a time to meet him and his band at their rehearsal place. We did, and we decided to join together. The name of their band was called Elite. In this band there was D.D. and Chubby, two guitar players, Kevin Tyler, the bass guitarist, and David was the drummer.

We were really cooking as we practiced and practiced some more. We were ready for the show, our very first real concert by ourselves.

CHAPTER 6

The First Concert as Superior Movement

Bottom left to right: Kevin, David, D.D.
Top left to right: Calvin, Billy, Stanley, David, and Tyrone

Yes, this was it. We had a chance to do a show by ourselves. However, I don't think we got paid for it. We were just anxious about doing a show of our own. To top it off, this show was outside. It was at a block club party on the 4300 block of Cullerton. A day before the show, we got our uniforms together. You guessed it! Back to Maxwell Street we went. This time we bought some powder blue pants with two straps to hold them up. We also bought white shoes with heels about three inches tall. As I look back, it's a trip. I can't believe we wore stuff like that. To top it off, we wore those same old pink, ruffled, Tom Jones-looking shirts! We were ready.

On the day of the concert, we agreed to change our name. Since the band's name was Elite and our old name was the Fourth Movement (before David), we decided to combine names. Elite meant Superior, so we kept Movement and added Superior to our first name. We became "Superior Movement." Actually, we and the band were like one. We were called The Superior Movement Singers and they were called The Superior Movement Band.

Anyhow, the next day came. It was showtime. We were ready. A lady who lived on the block let us get dressed in her house. The band began playing. We were checking each other out, making sure everyone's uniform fit. They were all right except they were too colorful. If this was your first time seeing us and you didn't know us, you would have sworn up and down that we were five gay spiritual singers with all those bright colors.

By the way, the bottoms of our pants were so wide you could hardly see our shoes. Yeah! That's right. Back then the elephant style was in. This was right before bell bottoms came out. To tell you the truth, I didn't see how we could have danced in those pants. Every time we made a move, the pants would flap! Just like elephant ears! Like wings, I would say!

Anyhow, we came running out. Some of the crowd was clapping while the others were laughing. Hey, we didn't care; we were getting ready to do our thing. Billy gave us the signal to start singing. Then we started to do our dance routine. As soon as we made a move, microphone stands began to fall down. Instead of putting the microphone cords away from the area we were dancing in, someone put them directly in the way. So where we were dancing, there were five cords stretched out across the ground. No, there wasn't even a stage! We had to sing and dance in the street. How does Little Richie say it—dancing in the streets? Well, it's true. There were potholes and cracks everywhere, let alone the microphone cords. But hey, the show must go on! Nothing stopped Superior Movement! We sang, and we danced. At the beginning of the show, we had five microphones, because there were, of course, five singers. By the end of the show, there was only one microphone standing. The others had fallen down. Either someone had tripped over a cord or someone did a spin and knocked them down. Nevertheless, there was only one microphone standing. As a matter of fact, it didn't matter anyway, because half of the microphones we were singing in hardly worked! They sounded like you were singing through a CB transmitter radio or something. You should have been there; you would have had the laugh of your life! We didn't know how we were going to get out of this one. Thank God, Baby wasn't there!

Now that I look back, I can't believe it! We kept on singing and dancing like nothing was happening. Finally Billy or Tyrone walked off stage and the rest of the group followed. The band didn't know what to do. They started to play the next song, thinking we were going to come back out! No way! Enough was enough. I think we had enough for one day. They finally got the message and came inside.

Now that the show was over and a mess, we were scared to go home. No one wanted to come outside. You know how it is when you do a concert. After every concert, someone is always hanging around to tell you how good or bad you were. In our case, we were terrible. The show was a complete flop. So there we were, wondering who was going out first. Again Billy led the way, and we followed. Back to the basement we went.

We were back at home now, back in Junior's basement, that is. We sat down and started to argue. What in the heck went wrong? We didn't know who to blame it on. We knew that we did our part and the band did their part. But somebody had to accept the blame. Therefore, we blamed it on the band. They should have checked the microphones before we came out. They also shouldn't have put the cords around the area where we were performing. There also should have been a stage. So we put it all on the band.

We had conflicts for a while, but we laid it all to rest afterward. We apologized to the band and began rehearsing again. We even laughed about it. A week later, we had another show coming up. This was getting serious! And guess where this show was going to be? That's right ... Farragut High School!

Since things were getting serious, we needed a manager. We agreed to let Mrs. Tyler manage us. Mrs. Tyler was our bass player's mother. She was a very nice lady. See, I don't talk bad about everybody! Mrs. Tyler treated all of us like her very own, so we called her "Mom." Whenever we would rehearse at her house, she would be glad to give us milk and cookies. Sometimes she would even offer us cold cut sandwiches. So by us rehearsing under adult supervision, we had to leave the shake and bake alone. There was no alcohol allowed in our new rehearsal place, which was in the attic of Mrs. Tyler's home. So at first we were down in a basement, then we moved up, up into an attic, and now we were getting ready for a show at Farragut High School.

CHAPTER 7

First Concert at Farragut High

FARRAGUT HIGH SCHOOL, CHICAGO, ILLINOIS

Well, here we were again! We were making progress. Just think, we used to have to audition to get into talent shows at Farragut. Now they were willing to pay us for doing a whole show! That was great! I can remember it so well. This show was important to all of us. This was a chance to make up for the last outside concert. A lot of students from Farragut were there. They lived on Mrs. Tyler's block, so we knew they were coming just to laugh. However, the joke was on them this time. We performed, and we got down. We made no mistakes whatsoever. We had a friend M.C. the show. His name was Cordell Jackson, and we paid him to make sure all the microphones were working. He was to make sure that no cords would be in the way so that we could do our dance routines.

Before Cordell announced us to the audience, he told a few jokes. Evidently they were bad jokes, because someone threw a garbage can on stage while he was telling them. That was a clue to him to get the show on the road. Finally he did. He announced Superior Movement, and we came running out. The audience was screaming and clapping. We were cleaner than the board of health. This time we wore tuxedos! The only bad thing I have to say about our uniforms this time is that we wore those same old pink ruffled shirts. It seemed like we just couldn't get rid of them! No matter what kind or color pants we wore, we had to wear those pink shirts! We got rid of the Tom Jones pink ruffled shirts after hearing some friends and fans speak the truth about them. They were gone just in time for our next show.

The show at Farragut was a success. Everything went well. This gave us more inspiration and determination to stay together as a group. We began to get more respect from people around the school and neighborhood. They seemed to be enjoying what we were doing.

The group members grew closer to each other. I'm not saying we weren't close already, but what I am saying is that we all had friends outside of the group that we hung around with when we weren't rehearsing. We began to spend less time with those friends and hung around each other more. I think the friends we had at that time understood what we were trying to do. I say this because they are still around today, and when they saw us somewhere, they would ask us, "When is the next show?" or "When will the next record be released?" We would always say "Soon," or "It's coming," but usually not knowing when.

Things began to get better and better for the group. We were even beginning to get phone calls for shows. I couldn't believe it. Every other weekend we had a show. We began to do shows in night clubs and hotels throughout the city of Chicago. Whenever we weren't doing a show at Wee Willies on a weekend, we had somewhere else to perform. Speaking of Wee Willies, let me tell you about this place. This book wouldn't be complete if I didn't tell you a little about Wee Willies.

Wee Willies was a night club about two blocks away from Farragut. It seemed like every time we did a show, it was at Wee

Willies! If the students looked old enough, they could get in sometimes to see the show. This went on for a while until the place closed down. I kind of believe Wee Willies closed down because of us. I might be wrong, but this is my opinion. What happened was we had just agreed to stop letting Mrs. Tyler manage us. We didn't think she was fair when she bought her son Kevin a bass amplifier with our money without our permission. So we decided to leave her and let David's sister, Bonnie, manage us. We also had another band to play behind us. Anyway, we did the show, and it turned out to be a lousy show. The owners of the place got into an argument that night because one wanted to pay us and the other didn't. They were husband and wife. The wife said the show was terrible, and the husband said we still played and we should get paid. So as it turned out, we didn't get paid.

We had no way to get our equipment home. The guy who brought the equipment to the show heard through the grapevine that we weren't getting paid, so he went home. As it turned out, we ended up carrying the equipment ourselves. Everybody grabbed a piece of equipment and either dragged or carried it to Bonnie's basement. Bonnie lived about a mile away from Wee Willies. It must have been about 2:30 in the morning as we carried the equipment home. Everything seems so clear now. As we were walking in the streets with the equipment, we saw a body lying in the street. Everybody was wondering if we should stop to see if he was dead or not. We decided to see. Someone shook him, and he moved. He smelled like alcohol. As soon as we knew he was alive, we got the heck away from there. Besides, we were in a Hispanic neighborhood. We wanted to get home.

David's sister Bonnie allowed us to rehearse in her basement for about two to three months. Then her husband Willie James began to complain because the light bill was beginning to rise. They didn't mind us rehearsing there, but we had to start paying rent. The amplifiers and speakers were pulling too much energy, and Bonnie and Willie James couldn't afford to pay a higher electricity bill. So we had to make another move. Where? We didn't know, but we had to do something. We discussed it, and we met this guy named Pedro. Pedro said he would manage us and we would be able to pay rent.

He said he would get us enough shows and that we wouldn't have any problems.

So now Pedro was our manager. He sold fruit out of his van to make a living. When he wasn't selling fruit, he would use the van to move our equipment to and from shows. If I can recall, I think we only did one or two shows with Pedro being our manager. After he found out that we used to eat his fruit on the way to our shows, he deserted us. He left without saying anything. Come on! We couldn't have been that bad. Now what!

Well, it was time to look for another manager. We looked and looked. Finally we found someone, and wouldn't you believe it! It was Mr. Powell, Tyrone's father. He said he could get us shows and that we wouldn't have to worry about paying rent. Well, we gave him a shot at it. Mr. Powell took us to one audition. After that, all we did was rehearse. No shows. Soon after this, Mr. Powell started to ask us to pay rent.

CHAPTER 8

Smitty As Manager
aka
Christian Smith

"SMITTY"

Mr. Powell said his electric bill was going up enormously. So we agreed to pay the rent out of our pocket. He didn't charge us much, but it was enough, since none of us had jobs. So we continued to rehearse and at the same time looked for another manager. Billy had a guy named Christian Smith in mind. Everybody called him "Smitty." He told us about Smitty, and we began to check him out. Christian was a guy who was in his late fifties at the time. He used to be Michael's manager a couple of years back. He also worked as the head janitor at William Penn Elementary School. This is the school most of us attended when we were younger. Smitty was a very wise man. He was so wise that we almost couldn't convince him to manage us. At first we would go up to the school every day just to push him into managing us. He kept on rejecting us. Finally he took a chance. He came to see us rehearse. He liked what he saw. He came back the following week and brought us one microphone. Imagine one microphone for five guys. Now is that cheap or what? I guess he didn't want to spend too much money too fast. He probably wanted to make sure we were serious.

After Smitty realized we were serious in what we were doing, he bought four more microphones. He told us to get a band together because it was time to get down to business. So we did just that. But then another problem came along. Mr. Powell wanted more money for rent. We didn't have it. We told him that Smitty would take care of everything, and of course he did. Smitty told us that we could now rehearse in the basement of the building that he owned. This building was located on 16th and Ridgeway. We took all our equipment to 1655 S. Ridgeway.

We put a new band together because we knew what it would take for us to sound good. This time our band had a bass player named Tyrone Collins, Lany, a guitar player who only knew about four chords, David Glover, a drummer, Chubby, another guitar player, and Wayne Hill, who played guitar and keyboards. So now we were kicking. Smitty had us performing everywhere in Chicago. We were beginning to do shows even in the South suburbs. With Smitty, things began to happen. Shows, shows, and more shows!

Most of our shows were performed on the south side of Chicago. Let me tell you about some of them. You wouldn't believe some of the things that happened. First of all, we did an audition for a talent show at Operation Push—Jessie Jackson's place, yeah! Okay, after we performed the audition, then they turned around and said that we

SMITTY'S FAMILY REUNION IN ALABAMA
Left to right: Smitty, David, Stanley, Calvin, Billy,
Greg, Tyrone, Lamont, Marty, and Wayne

were too good to participate in the talent contest. Then offered for us to be in the show but not as contestants. So Smitty said we should do it to get the publicity. I remembered this line so well, because we've done a lot of shows for publicity.

Next, we did another audition at a club in Harvey. The club was called Mr. Lee's. We used to play there regularly until the owner found out that we were drinking the orange juice and beer that he had in storage. This would have never happened if he would have given us a real dressing room and not his storage room.

Another show that I'll never forget was a show at a club called The Ghetto Lounge. This place looked like its name. It was located on Maxwell Street. The only reason we did a show here was because Tyrone's mother got the show. We did it as a favor for her. Smitty usually had us play in very respectable places. This time was an exception. Anyhow, we did an hour-long show and packed up. We didn't waste any time trying to get out of this place. So just as we began to take the equipment out of the place, two hard-looking guys had entered the door. They saw us about to leave and stopped us. They said they wanted to see a show. Smitty told them the show was over. They said they paid their money, and they wanted to see a show. Smitty went to talk to Mrs. Collins to give them their money back. She refused. She said she wasn't worried because she had a big gun in her purse. The two guys wouldn't let us go. One of them put his hand under his coat and said he wanted to see a show. So Smitty told us to get back up and sing. We did. We must have sung for two more hours, and we sang good!

After doing several shows, we began to buy our own sound system together. We also bought the band new equipment. It was hard because we wanted to get paid, too! Every time we were saving to buy something, Smitty would say, "Fellas, you have to sacrifice if you want to make it." As soon as we bought David Glover a new drum set, he quit the group. He said his mother didn't want him to play in the band anymore. David took the drums and vanished for a while. Smitty's favorite line back then was sacrifice. We also bought Tyrone Collins a new bass guitar. He didn't quit until later. David Glover was replaced by several drummers. A guy named Lucas played for a while, and then a guy named Mike took his place.

Mike was a very interesting drummer. He was a very quiet guy. He wouldn't say much at rehearsal. The most unusual thing about Mike was that he would always throw a drum stick at one of the singers as we rehearsed. We would be in the middle of a song and a drum stick would come flying through the air. At first we thought he was just joking, but then it happened again and again. What really made it come to our attention was when he did it at a show. It's the truth. This guy threw a drum stick at one of us at a show. It didn't hit anyone, but it just nicked someone's head. Finally Mike had to leave. Enough was enough! He was replaced by Marty Sias. After Tyrone Collins, the bass player left, he was replaced by Jessie Williams.

So as the years progressed, we also progressed. We were buying everything to improve our group. We had about five or six different uniforms, a good sound system with monitors, brand new microphones—anything dealing with band equipment, we had it. Everything we had was brand name. We had equalizers, power amps, and a twenty-four-channel P.A. board; we had all of this because we did as Smitty said, "Sacrifice and save our money." After a while it was getting too hard to sacrifice because we were getting older. The older you get, the more responsibilities you have, and the more money you're going to need. Things were getting tough.

We continued to do shows. We entered several talent contests as well. Every talent show that we entered, we came in first place. All the events prior to then had occurred between 1974 and 1977. Now we were all out of high school except David Williams, who had about another year to go. We auditioned for a talent contest at Dallas Entertainment Center on the south side of Chicago. This was one of the top live entertainment clubs in Chicago at that time. If we came in first place in the talent contest, we could open up for the stars that would be appearing there. We did just that. We won, and we opened up for the Dramatics, Enchantment, and several more top vocal groups back then. We were learning a lot just by being at the shows with these artists. Another show I won't forget was a show we did at the Southern Lounge in Harvey, Illinois.

OUR NEW BAND
Top left to right: Jessie, Lucas, Wayne
Bottom left to right: Our horn section, Dwayne, Aridus

Every time we performed there, we would get a crowd. One particular night we went to the dressing room to rest because we had a second show the same night. While we were in the dressing room, the security guard who was supposed to be protecting us grabbed David Williams by the neck. He was mad because David had sung to his girlfriend. Luckily, Jessie, our bass player, came in and made him leave. After all, Jessie is about six-foot-three and 210 pounds. This goes to show you that this business isn't easy.

WE REHEARSED IN THIS BASEMENT
FOR FIFTEEN YEARS.

We began to do more shows. We even put on shows for ourselves. Every year we would do an anniversary show to help buy equipment or uniforms for the group. In a lot of our shows, we would have shake dancers. This was Smitty's specialty. He loved to have a shake dancer at the show with us. Yes indeed, Superior Movement was on the move! We began to do shows on local TV stations. People were writing about us in local newspapers. Everybody in town was beginning to notice Superior Movement.

CHAPTER 9

Summertime of '78

AT A LOCAL T.V. STATION
Left to right: Dwayne (trumpet player), David, and Billy

Since we weren't nationally known yet, Smitty decided it was time to make another move. I guess people were telling him, "If you want to get discovered, you will have to leave Chicago." So that's exactly what we did. We went on a mini tour to New York and Washington DC. We were supposed to appear at the Apollo Theater in New York, but we didn't make it there in time. However, we did play in a hotel and also at the world-famous Cotton Club in Harlem. There was only one small problem. There weren't many people in the audience. We also visited several radio stations while we were there.

We then went to New Jersey to visit some of Smitty's relatives. Later on that night, I dropped a glass or something, and everybody was saying that I was drunk. This really made me mad, because I knew I wasn't. So when we got back to the hotel that we were staying in, I didn't say anything to anyone. I was still mad. A couple of the guys tried to get me to go out for a walk with them. I refused. So they went out and ended up watching a live X-rated show. How they got in, I don't know. We all were underage at that time.

A couple of days later, we traveled to Washington DC. By the way, we were traveling throughout the town in a van and a trailer and there were eleven of us! Can you imagine eleven people in one van? We were cramped the whole time, but we managed.

PREPARING TO LEAVE FOR TOUR IN '78
Left to right: Smitty, Billy, Calvin, Wayne, Tyrone, Stanley, Dwayne, Aritus, Lamont, Lucas, and Jessie

Just chillin'
left to right: Wayne, Jessie, Stanley, and Lucas

TYRONE

When we got to Washington, we didn't have the reservations we thought we had. So we had to go across the street to another hotel. We went to view the town. We spotted the street where the hookers worked. So later on that night, we went back to that same street. We went to bother them, and they gave us a piece of their minds. The hookers told us to get the heck out of there. After all, we were young teenagers having fun. After they chased us away, we went back to our hotel. We decided to go swimming the next day. The hotel we stayed at had a huge swimming pool. We couldn't all swim but, everyone got into the pool. First Calvin dived off the diving board. Then Lucius, at that time our drummer, dived in. Then I, knowing I wasn't a good swimmer, dived in too, trying to be like Calvin and Lucius. However, I sunk straight to the bottom of the pool. I came up standing on my tiptoes. I could hardly say anything because I became very nervous. Lucius noticed the expression on my face and came to help me. That was a relief, and I never got back into the pool after that.

Later on that day, we all started to complain because we didn't have anymore money. I don't know how all the money had disappeared so fast. No, I take that back, I do know! On our way to New York, we stopped at several restaurants. Everybody was ordering too much to eat. Every time we ate somewhere, there was always food left over. So by the time we got to New York, Smitty started to slow down on spending. We were now on a budget. That's right. Smitty came up with the term "Continental Breakfast." Every time we ate, it would be milk and donuts or a cold cut sandwich and pop.

HIGHWAY STOP ON THE ROAD
Left to right: Stanley, Tyrone, Calvin, and Billy

SUPERIOR MOVEMENT IN NEW YORK

While we were in Washington, we all called home and told our parents to send us some money because we were broke. This continental breakfast mess was getting out of hand. After our money arrived, we did our last show, and then back home we went. The whole tour was exciting; however, we didn't get what we wanted. We were really hoping someone big would see us.

So, there we were back in Chicago, and we started to do more and more shows. Somehow we got in touch with Ben Branch. He was a well-known alderman, and he was in charge of special events for Chicago. We did several shows for him, including some neighborhood festivals. We even did a show at the Band Shell. The Band Shell was a popular stage located in downtown Chicago. It is located on the lakefront and on the grounds of Grant Park. There must have been at least three thousand people out there. This was the biggest crowd we'd ever performed for at that point. It was a success; however, out of all those people who were there, no record company or producer had approached us. After this, we continued on. Shows were constantly coming up.

Photo Shoot

Chapter 10

Getting a Record Contract

We finally ran into some luck the next year. I was in college and was taking a mini course in producing on the weekend. My instructor was a professional guitar player named Bobby Robinson. He was telling the class that there was going to be a seminar downtown about the record industry. He said it would be a good idea if we attended the seminar. I didn't go, but I told Smitty about it and he went. He took along a tape of some of our original tunes we had done in the past. He met this guy named Tarice White. Tarice was the son of Danville White. Danville White worked at CBS for thirty-something years. He was about to retire, so they gave his son Tarice $100,000 to start his own record company. This was all a favor for Danville. Before this, Tarice was a marketing agent for a major record company. So he had been in the business prior to the record company.

When Tarice heard the tape of our originals, he kind of liked the group. He then wanted to see us perform. He came to one of our shows and loved it. The show that Tarice came to was a show we did at the Dallas Entertainment Center on the south side of Chicago. We were doing one of our anniversary shows. I think we really blew his mind, because we blew our minds that night! We had just done a show in Iowa prior to this. There was another young group on the stage with us (Stardom). Anyway, we were supposed to have been the stars of the show, but Stardom, a group of young guys, came on stage and rocked the place. They had everyone moving and grooving.

STANLEY

They even had Andrews, who was our sound man, working the lights for them! They were excellent!

We had to come on behind these guys. We really didn't want to, because we had on three-piece suits. The crowd was exhausted after Stardom left the stage. So we went out there and did the show. It was okay, but we knew we had gotten up-staged.

So the following week at the Dallas Entertainment Center, we had invited Stardom to do the show with us again. We knew how tough it would be if we didn't come up with something quick. So we

39

decided to have rehearsal every day. Everyone was to be at rehearsal at 7:00 sharp. We were not going to let a group of young teenagers up-stage us at our own anniversary show. No way! So we practiced and practiced. We had to think of gimmicks to put in our show. We had to come out of those three-piece suits, and we did just that.

Showtime it was. First Stardom came out. They were good. All of our friends and family were wondering what we were going to do. They loved Stardom. They didn't expect us to do a better job than them. But ha! Ha! We did!

First we turned all the lights off in the building. Then we came out on the stage with the band. No one could see us yet because it was pitch black. We had on brand-new white outfits. We were standing on some square blocks so that we could be on different levels. When the band started to play a rumble sound, fog began to fill the stage.

TYRONE

Smoke was all over the stage. The crowd was screaming and clapping with amazement. They didn't expect this. Then the lights came on, and we jammed. We tore the house up. After the show, our dressing room was so crowded we could hardly get dressed. All our friends and relatives and fans were in our dressing room. Everyone was congratulating us. We felt so proud.

After the show, Tarice was convinced that we were his group. He was very impressed. He decided to sign us to his new label. It was named CIM, standing for Chicago International Music. We were the first group to sign on this label. At first I didn't think we were going to get signed at all. I say this because there was so much confusion with the contract. A lot of it we couldn't understand, so we had to hire a lawyer. At first we ended up with the same lawyer CIM had, so we had to get another lawyer. Then we ended up with Dr. Rubin. He explained to us that the contract wasn't in our favor. He also said it was good if we just wanted a record out, but we just needed to remember that it wasn't written in our favor. One thing we didn't like at all was the fact that CIM wanted possession of our name, Superior Movement. This was important to us. We didn't want the company to own the name Superior Movement. This meant that if we ever left the record company, the record company could start another group with the name Superior Movement.

We argued this point to CIM, and they finally agreed to let us keep our name. We continued to discuss and argue until we received an agreement to sign. The moment we signed, things began to look up for us. We were now beginning to go back and forth into the studio. We even stayed until 5:00 in the morning sometimes. Soon after recording several tunes, our first record was being played on the radio. We couldn't believe it! At first they would play it early in the morning or late at night. This was a tune written by the late Van McCoy. It was titled "For You." We revised it and took a line from the Temptations' tune "My Girl" and mixed it in the song. It was all right, but the group didn't want CIM to release that particular tune. We told them that people wouldn't buy it. We didn't think it was a good tune to release, but we didn't have any say so.

DAVID

As it went, "For You" was getting more and more air time on the radio. Most of the members of the group would turn their radios up loud as they could whenever "For You" was playing. Things were really going well for us. We made a lot of personal appearances at local record stores. Every time we went somewhere, people were asking for our autographs. We also were invited to all the top discos in Chicago and Milwaukee to pantomime our records. It was fun! Fun! Fun! Superior Movement was spreading out throughout the Midwest.

After "For You" had died down, we began to get ready for the studio again. We went over one of Tarice's friend's house to listen to some tunes they wanted us to record. This friend of Tarice was a producer by the name of Don Burnside. He was pretty popular in the music industry. Anyway, when we heard the songs, we didn't like them. CIM got upset. We took the tapes home, but we didn't rehearse on them. We found it very difficult to sing something we had no feelings for.

BILLY

So later on, Tarice called Smitty and told him we weren't cooperating. Smitty told us to just do the song and cooperate. We rehearsed on the song several times. Then, after Burnside went to the studio to lay the music down, the song sounded a little better. Some of the guys in the group liked it, and some still didn't have any feeling for it. Anyhow, the tune, "Wide Shot," was released. It was playing on the radio every time you looked around. It did very well on the charts. Superior Movement was cooking. We were doing a lot of outside concerts during the summer of '83. Every time we made an appearance somewhere, we would come in a limousine. We were treated like real stars. Well, at least sometimes. I say this because we did a show with the Dramatics one day. The club we were playing at had two dressing rooms. We didn't know which dressing room was ours or which dressing room was for the Dramatics, so we chose one. The room we chose had a plate with all kinds of fruit and meat and bottles of champagne on the side. It was very clean and neat. We couldn't believe that all this was for us; it wasn't! They told us that we were in the wrong dressing room. Our dressing room was across the hall. So we went across the hall, and there it was, a plain little old dressing room. They had orange juice for us and that's it—no meat or champagne.

CIM had us do a lot of shows for publicity. They said it was important for us to do these shows because a lot of important people would be there, and they needed to see us. So we went along with it. We were doing shows at expensive hotels. We even went to Georgia to do a show at a big-time convention. We were on stage with Eddie Murphy. He wasn't as big as he is now. At that time, he was on Saturday Night Live every weekend. Anyway, Tarice made us stay backstage the whole time during the concert. We kept asking Tarice, "When will we go on stage?" He kept telling us to wait. Wait! Wait for what? There were all kinds of celebrities in the audience.

CALVIN

I mean, here was our chance to perform in front of the top entertainers in the United States—Stevie Wonder, the S.O.S. band, Carl Carlton, and George Clinton. Many more stars were right there in the very same room in which we were about to perform. It was getting late, and the affair was coming to a close. The M.C. was thanking everyone for coming. We still hadn't gone on stage yet. We were waiting for Tarice, who wasn't around. Everybody in the place was leaving. Finally Smitty got up and told somebody we were supposed to perform. The M.C. had finally announced us, but by this time half of the people were gone. They were all headed to the after set, which was held upstairs in the same hotel.

We really sounded good that night, I must admit. We also had a girl appearing with us. Her name was Evon Gage. She sang on one of the tunes with us from our album. CIM flew her to the concert, but they made us take the bus. So we made up for what they did. When it was time to order breakfast the next morning, we *ordered* breakfast! Our bill was sky high, but we didn't care, because CIM was footing the bill. After all, they could have treated us a little better than they did. So after we ate, back to Chicago we went.

We had to get ready for a photo session at McCormick Inn. We also had to get ready for work. Yep! All of us had eight-hour jobs, because we weren't making enough money to quit our jobs. So everyone had gotten off work the following Monday, and we were supposed to show up at the McCormick Inn. Tarice got mad because some of us were a little late.

New On The Charts

SUPERIOR MOVEMENT
For You—⭐

Superior Movement is a five-piece group from Chicago's West Side, whose members met and formed the group at Farragut High School. The lineup comprises Billy Avery, Calvin Ford, Tyrone Powell, Stanley Ratliff and David Williams. Powell doubles as the act's choreographer.

"For You," penned by the late Van McCoy, is the quintet's first recording, and also the first chart entry for Chycago International Music (CIM), which is marketed, manufactured and distributed through the Epic/Portrait/Associated Labels arm of CBS.

CIM was formed earlier this year by Maurice White, who has been active in independent promotion, management and publishing in the Windy City (Billboard, Aug. 1). He's the son of Granville White, associate national director for special markets at CBS Records.

Superior Movement originally sent White a tape of their work, but he displayed little interest until viewing their stageshow at Chicago's Copper Box Club. Impressed by that—White says the group reminds him of the early Temptations—he signed them to CIM, producing their debut disk himself.

The aggregation is currently working on an album for November release, and will tour nationally early in 1982. They have already appeared in clubs and hotels in and around Chicago, and in Washington, D.C. and New York.

Superior Movement is managed by Christian Smith, P.O. Box 14524, Chicago, Ill. 60614 (312) 737-5847.

We weren't that late, maybe twenty to twenty-five minutes, but what could we have done? He wasn't paying us enough to miss work that day. We began posing and posing. I didn't realize it would take all night. They wanted to have a good picture for the album cover. We must have taken at least five hundred snapshots that night. We posed in all kinds of positions, and if you saw the album cover, you wouldn't believe they picked the picture they did. To us, they picked one of the worst. Again, we didn't have any say so.

LIVE AT THE DALLAS ENTERTAINMENT CENTER
Left to right: Calvin, Billy, Tyrone, and David

The following week we did a show at a club on the south side. After the show, Tarice came into the dressing room to show us how the album cover would be. He was hoping that we would jump for joy, but we didn't. We didn't because on the back of the album where the artists thanked the people who helped them, we didn't get a chance to do that. Instead, Tarice thanked all his friends and relatives. We didn't get a chance to thank one person. Also, on the front of the album, all of our faces were the same color. Now we had light, brown, and dark-skinned people in the group. But on the album, all our complexions were the same. When Tarice found out we weren't so thrilled, he left. Don't get me wrong—we appreciated that we finally were getting an album out. We were super glad about this. It was just the way things were being done with CIM.

Left to right: Calvin, Stanley, Tyrone, and David

Chicago Defender

BILLY AND STANLEY

CHAPTER 11

Shoot Outs During Concert

Let me tell you about the shootings that occurred during some of our concerts. That's right, I didn't stutter at all. We actually did concerts where there was live gunfire. I can't believe it myself, but it really did happen—more than once, I must say. We thank God that no one in the group got hurt.

The first time it happened was at a club on 93rd and Ashland, "The Club." We played here at least once a month. One night two guys got into a fight while we were performing. After the fight was over, one of the guys left and said he would be back. We continued doing the show as if nothing had happened. The reason I remember this show so well was because this same night, the hostess had set five glasses of water on the stage in front of us.

The platform of the stage was low, so when she set the water down, everyone could see where she placed them. As the show went on, Calvin was singing his little heart out. He was so much into the song that he stepped right on top of the five glasses of water. Would you believe he didn't notice what he had done? It was hilarious. The other four of us were cracking up. Calvin just kept on singing.

By the time this was over, the guy who had left the fight had come back. He fired four to five shots in the window. Everybody in the place hit the floor. All the lights went off, and everybody on stage dove to the floor. All the ladies in the house were either screaming or crying. It stayed like this for about ten minutes. Then the lights came back on. The owner of the place apologized to everyone and then closed the place down for the night. Boy did we have something to talk and joke about even though one of us could have gotten shot!

During this time, we would always go back to the rehearsal place and help the band unload their equipment. This was something the singers didn't like at all. But Smitty, our manager, made us agree to do this. After all the sweating, singing, and dancing, we still had to carry equipment after a show. We were led to believe that this was all the part of sacrificing, as Smitty would say.

You would think that after doing the show at The Club, we wouldn't go back. But no, we were hard-headed. The very next month we went right back to The Club to perform. And guess what? The same exact thing happened. Someone shot inside The Club again. This time someone got shot, and the place was closed down for good.

We then did a show for W.G.C.I. Yes indeed! We were ready. There must have been ten thousand people out there. It was the summer of 1982. While we were singing, again we heard shots. People began to run everywhere. Little children were being trampled over. The people who were panicking seemed to have lost their grill and meat. It was awful, and to make it worse, the people that started it were all teenagers. They were mostly in gangs. One gang would be fighting another gang. This would make the other people that were watching the show run also. This created a stampede. The fence that was put up to separate the backstage from the audience was no longer there. The crowd had torn it down. Little babies were also getting trampled over. If a person that wasn't in a gang had on gang colors or his hat was turned to a certain side, the gang members would jump on him.

Once again the show had to be stopped because of the shooting. So off the stage we went. Again God was on our side. None of us got hurt. We had been pretty lucky so far, but again it happened. This time it was in another club. We had gone to the Southern Lounge in Harvey, Illinois, to receive an award. This award was given to us for being the best local vocal group in Chicago. The Chilites, which was a national singing group, were also there. After the Chilites had come off stage, we went on stage to pantomime our record. Before we could finish, there were shots fired. Everybody in the place hit the floor. All you could hear was glass being broken and people hollering and screaming. I didn't really know what was going on. The place was jam-packed. Bodies were everywhere, and the police came in about ten minutes later. The place was shut down for the night. The next day we read in the paper that the El Ruckins gang had something to do with this. Someone had also gotten killed that night. Again we were lucky that it wasn't one of us. One thing that helped us from getting hurt at shows is that we stayed together. Everybody knew where everybody was most of the time.

CHAPTER 12

Our Fan Club

We even had a fan club when our album was released. Four girls came up to Smitty and asked him if they could start a fan club. They were Michelle, Robin, Linda, and Sandra. I never did know their last names. But they all were very sweet and dedicated to the group. They sold tickets, T-shirts, and buttons for us. They were very good supporters. They wouldn't let anybody talk bad about us. If someone in the group needed a favor, we could always depend on these young ladies. After a while, the fan club got even bigger. The only bad part about it was that the club was all females.

Soon a conflict occurred. The fan club would show up at our rehearsals and our girlfriends or wives wouldn't like it. It wouldn't have been so bad if it was just the singers, but we had a band too. Some of the guys in the band were married and some had girlfriends. So all together, that was nine females who were angry because of our fan club.

You could feel the animosity at our shows. Our wives and girlfriends would always try to get close to the stage. This is where our fan club would sit, and you could just feel the tension. I thought it was really funny. Some of our friends would tell us after the show how words were exchanged between our girlfriends and fan club. They would roll their eyes at each other. Things got even worse because then our fan club started calling our houses. They didn't mean any harm—at least, I don't think so—but our girlfriends and wives didn't appreciate this. I got kind of worried myself because every time the phone rang, it would be one of the fan club members. They were always throwing parties and playing cards. At first I would always want to go, but then I had to slow down because I knew my girlfriend didn't like the idea. The other guys in the group felt the same way. They were going through the same thing. Whenever the phone rang, I prayed it wasn't one of the fan club members, because I knew there would be an argument after I hung up. I think Billy had it the worst because he was the lead singer. Somehow girls would get his number even if it was unlisted. He used to get mad at us because he thought we had given it to them. He must have changed his number ten times within a year. So after the tenth time, Billy refused to give his number to us or Smitty. Things began to settle down later on, and Billy finally gave us his number again. As for the fan club, it died down too. The four girls who started it were still behind us. But everyone else who was in it was not around anymore. When we get another record out, I was sure we'd hear from them again.

About a month or two later, we did a show with Phyllis Hyman. Well, part of a show, that is. This show was on 87th, right off the Dan Ryan expressway. It was on the grounds of Johnson Publishing Company. As we were on stage singing, two of our microphones kept cutting off. The people could hardly hear us. Then we were asked to cut our show. We were supposed to have thirty minutes on stage to perform. We ended up with fifteen minutes. We couldn't even hear ourselves singing through the monitors. Almost every time we had a show with a bigger star, we always got a raw deal. Either the sound would mess up, or they would cut our show. I think they did it because they didn't want us to upstage the other artist. This is just my personal opinion. But it always happened to us.

The same thing happened when we opened the show at the Regal Theatre. We were on the stage getting down and all of the sudden, cut! We were expecting it, so we finished the last song out. A lot of times we never got a change to sing our hit record because it was always the last song we sang. So now whenever we had a big concert to do, we asked how much time we had, and we based the show on that time. Sometimes we would just plan to do three or four tunes to make sure we didn't go over the time allotted.

SUPERIOR MOVEMENT AT THE
CLUB—73RD & ASHLAND
Left to right: Stanley, Tyrone, Calvin, and Billy

CHAPTER 13

Our Equipment Got Stolen

Yes, it is true. Our rehearsal place was broken into twice. The first time it happened early in the morning. We had just gotten finished doing a show. Everybody had unloaded and gone home. All the equipment was still broken down because of the show. About 6:00 in the morning, my phone rang. We had a security alarm that rang a couple of our phones and the police station in case of a burglary. By the time we got there, half of our equipment was gone. We asked the people who lived upstairs if they heard or saw anything. They said no.

Immediately we started to accuse the young guy who lived in the building. We had to start somewhere. Calvin wanted to beat the kid up because he strongly believed he had something to do with it. We also accused the guys who stayed down the street from the rehearsal place. These guys had all kinds of speakers and D.J. equipment. How they got them, we didn't know. But we do know that none of them had jobs. So we suspected them also. About a year after this, one of our friends said he saw our name on one of the speakers in the guys' house just down the street. We couldn't do anything because we didn't know exactly where it was, and we didn't have a search warrant. Another one of our friends said he saw our name on a speaker at another group's show. Our equipment seemed to be everywhere but in the right place.

So it was okay. We didn't let the break-in stop us. No way! We were Superior Movement, and we were determined to keep going. So we started to save again. We began doing shows and building our equipment back up. We bought better equipment and microphones. We even had a lady manager to assist Smitty. She offered to buy a double drum set for Marty, the drummer, as long as we paid her back. We bought monitors, equalizers, and power amps. We had everything. Then it happened again, another burglary. This time we couldn't blame the kid upstairs because he didn't live there anymore. Wayne, our keyboard player, lived upstairs. He said he and his family didn't hear anything. This we couldn't believe, because whoever the burglars were, they took their time doing what they had to do. They unscrewed all the screws out of the speaker cabinets. Then they unscrewed the speakers out of the monitors and equalizer cabinets.

There must have been one hundred screws all over the floor. On top of that there were beer cans lying around. They were drinking beer as they were stealing our equipment! And do you believe no one heard them? They took everything but the drums. That's very peculiar, because the last time someone broke in, they didn't steal the drums either. Boy were we sick! We didn't know what was next. Finally, Baby Bass (the guy who used to laugh at us) said he knew where our equipment might be. Baby had some kind of connections with the local gang members, so he might have been telling the truth. He told Smitty that he could get our equipment back for us if we gave him $800. It was worth it, because it was about $2,000 worth of equipment that was missing. Can you imagine buying your own equipment back from someone who might have had something to do with the stealing of it? We didn't know for sure if Baby had something to do with it; we just wanted our equipment back.

CHAPTER 14

More Shows

We finally paid Baby Bass $800.00, and he gave us our equipment back. It was all in his apartment. We began to do shows again. We did a show for the Human Services program. It was outside on a very hot day. We were wearing our white tuxedos. When the band started to play, we came running out. One by one we came running. There was a pole in the way, so we had to run around it. Everybody went around it but Calvin. Can you believe this? Common sense should tell you if the person in front of you goes around something, you should follow. But not Calvin! Calvin tripped over the pole and did a roll in his white tux. He got up, dusted himself off, and came on the stage as if nothing had happened. We laughed and laughed throughout the whole show about what happened.

We then did a show in our own neighborhood. This show was in Franklin Park. The last time we did a show in our neighborhood was about five years prior to this. That show was outside in the back part of Marcy Center. It was something we tried to do on our own. The stage was small, and there wasn't much light out there. Somehow Calvin had hooked light bulbs around the stage. If you were just passing by, you would have sworn it was a used car lot. Anyway, we did the show, and it turned out to be a success, even though someone began firing shots and we had to end the show.

Left to right: Tyrone, Calvin, and David

Getting back to Franklin Park, we were very popular in our neighborhood. A lot of people came out to see us. Some had banners made. Others wore Superior Movement T-shirts. The only thing we regret about doing this concert is the money we got paid. Bill Henry, who was our Alderman, didn't want to pay us enough money. He would only offer us $400–$500. If we hadn't been thinking about the people in the neighborhood, we would never have done the show. Some of the people didn't have a ride to the shows we did outside of the neighborhood. Some couldn't afford to pay for tickets. The little kids in the neighborhood were too young to get into a lot of our shows. So this show was for all the people in the neighborhood. Every year we ended up doing a show in the summertime at Franklin Park. Mr. Henry still didn't want to pay us no matter how good we were. Instead of Bill Henry paying us more, he paid us less. Finally, one year he didn't even want us to be in it. He instead got several groups from the south side to do the show. He even offered to pay Cornel Abram $3,000 to do a show. We just couldn't understand why he did this. Everybody in the neighborhood was expecting us to do the show. When we didn't appear, a lot of our friends were disappointed.

We were too. Bill Henry was now on our enemy list. After all we'd done for him, he let us down.

Well, enough about Bill Henry and his Summerfest. We continued to do more fests for other Aldermen. We were having better success with shows. Everything was going great.

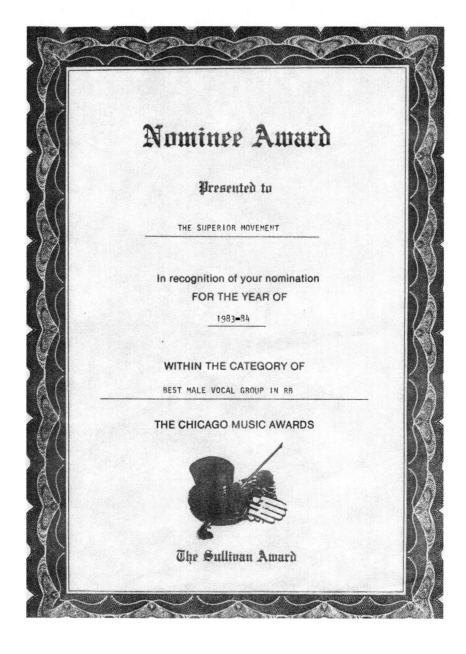

CHAPTER 15

Trouble with the Record Company

It was now time to complete the album. We had about four more tunes to do. When Don Burnside took us into the studio, he had us singing like birds. We sounded like a bunch of girls. Our harmony was extremely high. Even Tyrone sounded like a girl. So Billy told Burnside, "We're not a bunch of bitches!" Burnside got offended by this. He said, "That was a very derogative statement." After this, it seemed like everything was going bad for us. The company kept finding things to say and do about us. Next CIM told us that they wanted us to feature a girl on our album. They wanted us to do "Guilty" over. They said it was a classic, and it would cross over onto the pop chart. We told them that this was our first album, and we wanted it to just be us. At least give us a chance. But CIM insisted on doing the record. So what they did was take David in the studio and had him and Evon Gage do the lead singing. Then he had someone else do the background vocals. We didn't know what was going on. The next thing we knew, the album was out with "Guilty" on it, with Superior Movement not singing! This hurt us bad. We went to our lawyer to complain. Tarice had no right to do this, but the lawyer said it was too late. He said to go ahead since the album was completed. At least we had a hot record on the charts. We didn't want everything to stop all of a sudden. So then we brought up another situation. We asked the lawyer why CIM let someone else who was not in Superior

63

Movement sing a song on our album. How was it possible to get away with something like this? This was a real shocker. CIM had someone sing "Lost Affair." We didn't know who this guy was. Whoever it was, they couldn't sing any better than anyone else in the group. CIM repeatedly dogged us. They kept on retaliating against us. It was like they didn't want us to get better. They just wanted us to sing and let them do whatever they wanted to do.

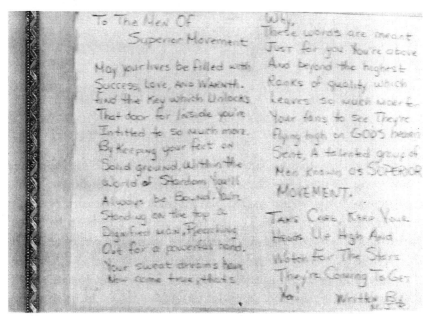

A LETTER FROM A FAN CLUB MEMBER

Another thing we didn't like was the fact that CIM didn't allow us to put one of our own tunes on the album, which we wanted to do at the time. We had a couple of tunes that could have been put on the album, but CIM never gave us a chance.

We kept going to our lawyer, hoping that he could solve the animosity between us. But things were getting worse. At first our record was moving fast up the chart. It started at number eighty-seven. Then the next week it was in the seventies. The third week it was in the sixties. It kept moving upward, but as we kept conflicting with CIM, all of a sudden it happened. Out of the clear blue sky the record dropped on the chart to number ninety-nine. It made it to number forty-seven, and all of a sudden it dropped in one week to ninety-nine. We couldn't believe it, but it really did happen. We asked Tarice what happened, and he never told us. Tarice began to lose all of his friends within the company. The friends he grew up with were no longer around. A guy by the name of Johnny Moore was helping Tarice when the company began. He was no longer there. We had gotten attached with Johnny around. When we found out that he had left, we knew something was up, but we never found out what.

Left to right: David, Billy, Calvin, Tyrone, and Stanley

As the record dropped and stopped playing on the radio, we kept asking Tarice what was happening. He never told us specifically; he would tell us anything he wanted just to get us out of his way. We used to call his home and work. He would never answer or return our phone calls. Again we went to our lawyer. Our lawyer contacted his lawyer and within weeks, Tarice called us. He said he had been working another job. Can you imagine that? This guy is supposed to be the president of our record company, and now he's saying he has another job as a factory worker! We couldn't believe it! Even to this day, I still don't believe it.

Anyhow, we went on with CIM and just let things flow. Tarice sent us a copy of a letter to CBS that stated CIM was dropping

Superior Movement. It said we were not cooperating with the company and that we refused to do our own material on stage. They said while taking pictures for the album, we were late and did not get along with the photographers. All these were lies, but we couldn't do anything about it. We didn't know exactly who Tarice sent this letter to. All we knew was that it was sent to someone at CBS.

If Tarice had invested money in the group, we could have been on our way. We could have made him and ourselves happy. All he had to do was believe in us and allow us to voice our opinion. Voicing your own opinion means a lot in this business. If you sit there and let someone tell you everything to do, or what moves to take, you'll be lost in the shuffle along with the other entertainers who don't know what they want. Tarice didn't even ask us which songs we felt they should release. It seemed like they didn't even care about us.

Although we have separated from CIM, we don't hold any grudges against them. This is the music business, and that's the way things are. We signed the contract, so we should have known what we were getting into. Who knows? Maybe one day in the future we'll team up with Tarice again. If so, believe me, things will be much different. So now we were no longer with a record company. Smitty said this was the best thing that could have ever happened to us. He told us not to worry. Somebody would be glad to sign us up. It wasn't that easy, however. We went on one, two, three years and still had no contract.

We had entered a talent showcase that was held downtown at one of the big hotels. It went on for the whole weekend. There were all types of seminars going on that talked strictly about the music business. There were seminars on how to break into the music business, how to be a songwriter, how to publish your songs, how to maintain a manager or a booking agent, and discussions of each of their duties. It told how records are pressed and released. They also had producers, lawyers, and A&R men give speeches on these topics.

The showcases were held in a separate section from the seminars. They had the seminars going on in the morning and the showcases beginning in the evening. We were hoping that a producer or a record company representative would get a glimpse of our act when we performed. Someone did see us. Some guy said he was from Philly

International. He said that he liked the group. He told us to send him a tape and he would tell his boss about us. We didn't have any tapes of our own material. We had original material, but it wasn't recorded on studio tape. They were done in the rehearsal place. Can you believe we had the gall to send the record company a tape like this? Smitty took a trip down there with a tape of our album and the tape we did at the rehearsal place. We were rejected. They told us to send a quality tape the next time.

Front: David
Left to right in back: Billy, Calvin, Tyrone, and Stanley

CHAPTER 16

Calvin Goes to the Army

Now that things were getting pretty rough for the group, we all had to think about ourselves much more. We had to think of what we were going to do if the group didn't make it. Everybody was getting frustrated. No shows meant no money. Rehearsals were getting very boring because we didn't have any shows to look forward to. It was also depressing at rehearsals because the microphones we were using began to get torn up. As a matter of fact, everything was getting torn up in the rehearsal place.

Calvin finally came out and said he was joining the army. He had made his mind up. Calvin didn't have a job, and all he was doing was hanging out on the streets until it was time for rehearsal. We understood what he was going through. We wished him the best of luck, and off he went. Calvin was now Uncle Sam's boy. Although Calvin left, we were still determined to keep the dream alive. Billy, Tyrone, David, and I were still hanging in there. We did a couple of shows here and there. We even did an anniversary show, and a lot of people couldn't believe Calvin had gone to the army. We really missed that high voice of his. Our fans also missed his voice. He could really hit those high notes at times. We won't talk about the time he couldn't quite hit some of those notes. You probably couldn't take it.

Things were getting even worse. We would always call Smitty and ask him what was up. He would always say, "Oh nothing." We eventually stopped calling Smitty, because he was always telling us that nothing was up. Well, we didn't exactly stop calling him. Every once in while we would just to stay in contact.

We kept rehearsing, just going with the flow. I can tell you there wasn't much of a flow, either. We did a summer fest every now and then. Gus Savage, our congressman, asked us to do his annual picnic. We did this for him about three or four years in a row, but we would never get paid. He always invited us to do a show on the S.S. Clipper at the end of every summer. Then he would pay us to do that show.

It had been about three or four months since Calvin left. He sent us a letter one day and told us how he was doing. He said that he liked it, but he couldn't stand taking orders from guys who were much younger than him. Let's face it, Calvin had been out of high school for about eight or nine years, so what did he expect, a silver platter? He said that he had gotten in a lot of trouble because he kept talking back to some of his superior officers who were younger than him.

About a month after Calvin sent us the letter, believe it or not, he was back in Chicago. He said that they had sent him home because of the leg injury he had. They were afraid that something might happen because the bone in his leg wasn't that strong. I forgot to mention Calvin's leg injury. A couple of months prior to Calvin joining the service, someone gave a party at our rehearsal place. This is how bad things were.

After the party, Calvin decided to walk home. He had been drinking spiked punch the whole night. It was very nice outside, so Calvin decided to walk home at 3:00 a.m. The next day about 9:00, everybody was calling my house saying Calvin was in the hospital. I rushed to the hospital to see how he was doing. He was all bandaged up from head to toe. His face was all swollen, and he had tubes tied to his penis. The boy was messed up. I asked him what happened! He said he was walking down Roosevelt and Cicero, and a car came and knocked him off the street. I asked him if he was sure he wasn't bothering anyone's lady! Or since he was near Cicero, I asked if he

was sure he wasn't flirting with one of the pimp's hookers! They do hang out around that area. He said no.

Calvin eventually got well and was reunited with the group. Now he was back, and Superior Movement had all five members again. But wait a minute! Now what? You've guessed it! Tyrone decided it was time for him to go.

CHAPTER 17

Tyrone Goes to California

Well I guess Calvin had his time to leave, so now Tyrone had to take his turn. Tyrone had just lost his job, and things were rough. Very few shows were popping up. Billy was singing with another group besides Superior Movement, but he still put Superior Movement first. Tyrone was fed up, and the only good thing to do was to go to California. His three brothers were out there and were doing well. So off he went. He must have called me every day. He said that while he was working at the airport, he was running into celebrities every day. He said he was missing the group. Every day at 7:30 he would think of the group, because that was the time we had rehearsed.

The group had a show at Mr. G's. We had to make up steps to songs because Tyrone wasn't there. We did, but they weren't the typical Superior Movement style. We had to do the best we could. We passed on the show. It was just all right.

We then had a show coming up at Chicago State University. They wanted one of the members to represent the group on a radio talk show. They didn't tell us enough time in advance, so none of us could take off work for the interview. We were lucky that Tyrone had called me the night before and told me he was on his way back to Chicago. I told him over the phone about the interview, and he said he would be there. That was a relief for us. It was good to hear his voice, especially on the radio, talking about the group. So once again, Superior Movement was back with all five members.

Superior Movement was back in full force. We continued to do shows, and every show we did was good. We were now putting more songs we wrote into our shows. At the same time, Smitty began looking for another manager for us. He said that he had taken us as far as he could, which he did. He gave us some really good times. I'm sure if it wasn't for him, we wouldn't have been together at that point. Smitty wanted us to check out two guys he had in mind to manage us. We had several meetings with these guys, but whenever we met, Calvin was not there. The proposed managers said that we should drop Calvin because they could see he wasn't as serious as the rest of us. Then they came to one of our shows and were pleased with our performance. After this, they began pressuring us to sign contracts.

We weren't in a hurry to sign because the contract they had was so difficult to understand. We'd learned our lesson from the contract we signed with CIM, so we took our time to review the contract. Just when we made up our minds that we were going to sign, another guy stepped in and said he would like to manage us. His name was Carl Lewis Jr. He had his own management company, called L.P.M. He explained what they were about and what exactly they could do for the group. His associates were as friendly as he was. Although they were young, they were two level-headed guys.

Carl Lewis had given us a contract and asked us to review it. His contract was much easier to understand than the other managers' contracts. He gave us plenty of time to review it. The one thing I like about what he said was that "in order for L.P.M. to make a million, Superior Movement has to make theirs first."

CHAPTER 18

Signing with L.P.M.

We were doing our last show with Smitty as our manager. It was at a hotel on New Year's Eve. We hadn't signed with L.P.M. yet, but Carl Lewis was our acting manager. Ruby Donahue was a lady we had done shows for since we started out. She wanted us to do the show for the same price that we had done seven or eight years ago. Then she wanted the band to play behind another group and wanted to set our rehearsal for us. Carl Lewis sent her a letter and told her that we are a much more advanced group now. She couldn't use our band unless she paid them extra, and he also told her *not* to plan rehearsal for us. We were impressed by what Carl did, so after New Year's Day, we signed the contracts. Superior Movement is now under the management of L.P.M. Smitty was still around us. We always kept in touch with him because, in a sense, he is one of us.

We began doing shows with Carl Lewis as our manager. Every show we had up to that point was a success. Then Calvin got sick. He was in the hospital for a month or two. During this time, we had shows coming up. So we ended up doing shows with just the four of us. When Calvin got out of the hospital, he said he needed a little time to get himself together. He said that he was still interested in the group, but he needed time off. So we said okay. We gave him plenty of time, but he wasn't Calvin anymore. He was keeping his distance from us. You know how someone may be in jail for a long time and when he gets out, he's a different person? Well, that is how Calvin was acting toward us. We even decided to hold rehearsal over at his house, but even this didn't work. Calvin wouldn't even show up. So Carl kept asking us, "What is Calvin going to do?" We kept telling him that Calvin would come through. So we kept on rehearsing, and Calvin slowly dropped out of the group. We couldn't convince him to stay in. So now it still stands—Superior Movement was Billy, David, Tyrone and me. We were doing better. We kind of tightened our act up. We tried to work more in the studio at Carl's house. Before then we weren't working on our own material as much. Carl introduced us to a young guy by the name of Pierre. This guy wrote great music. It was exactly what we'd been looking for. What he would do was write the music and allow us to put the lyrics to the songs. Everything was working out perfect. All we needed was someone to put the money behind us.

CHAPTER 19

Looking for a Deal

As I stated before, we were focusing on writing and producing our own material. We also had established our own publishing company. We sent three tunes to about fifteen record companies, and we had three or four letters saying that they couldn't use us at the time. We expected some rejection, so we were going to continue to write and produce. Right We were not giving up because we'd worked so hard already. Eventually someone would open their eyes and give us a chance. And when that chance did come, they wouldn't regret it!

Well, as you may or may not know, most of the band members were actually with Superior Movement for a long time. We grew up together. We'd been the best of friends for the longest time. All of a sudden, things began to change. We were still friends, but we didn't have the closeness that we used to have.

It all began when Smitty sold the building to Wayne, our keyboard player. For years we rehearsed in the basement of this building. We never had to pay rent. It was like a second home, yes indeed! Sixteenth and Ridgeway brings back sweet memories for Superior Movement and their followers. As months went by, all Superior Movement did was focus on recording and going into the studio. We were really preparing ourselves. At this point, we had about two whole albums of songs recorded. They weren't fully mixed, but they were laid out pretty good!

We did a couple of shows, but that was it. I would say that in 1987, we didn't do more than ten shows the whole entire year.

Our band was wondering what was up with us. They didn't seem to like our new manager. There was a conflict there, and I really don't know where or how to begin telling you about it. Yet I will try to explain it the best way that I can.

When Wayne became full owner of this building, he began charging us rent. Well, hey, we figured everything would be the same. Smitty sold the building, but we thought we still had a rehearsal place. This wasn't the case at all. All hell began to break out.

Wayne began charging us rent, and we had to pay. I mean, it was a shocker to us. It was his building, and he had the right to collect rent. The odd thing about this is that Wayne somehow had his electricity hooked up to the basement where we were, and guess what? That's right. We were now paying the light bills too. But hey, that's okay, we were Superior Movement. Anybody who wanted to use they did. I was not just Wayne. We had a few more friends who would get us into situations that we didn't have any control over. I wouldn't say that we were dumb, but we were just nice guys. Too nice!

Now getting back to the band. Since Wayne wanted to get paid for us using his rehearsal place, the rest of the band wanted to get paid after every show. I mean after every show, even if it was a benefit concert, our band wanted to get paid. There were times when we didn't get a penny, but you better believe the band got paid. On top of this, the band began to play behind other groups. So now you know what was going on. It became harder for us to practice in the basement, although we paid rent; we still had to wait for the band to finish rehearsing with the other groups. You would think that since we were there first, we should get the first option to rehearse first, but it wasn't like that at all. We, Superior Movement, would come at 7:30 to rehearse, but we wouldn't actually start until 11:00. Yes, yes, yes. I wouldn't lie to you.

Now how does that old saying go? "Nice guys finish last!" Well believe it—it's true. We'd be there all night waiting to rehearse. Just like Rodney Dangerfield, "No respect!" It was unbelievable! We were too damn nice: 1) We paid rent; 2) Wayne had the lights hooked up to the basement; 3) We couldn't rehearse because the band had other obligations; 4) The other groups even used our equipment for a while.

Those are just a few of the things that went on between us and the band. Our managers didn't like what was going on any better than we did. They kept telling us to get our equipment from down there. Our managers wanted us to get everything that belonged to us! This caused even more conflict because our band didn't want us to take the equipment. The whole year was chaos.

We eventually had all of our equipment removed from the basement. Okay, now what? Now "Superior Movement" didn't have a band. Carl said, "Don't worry about it." All we needed was a deal, and everything else would work out. At least that's what we thought.

CHAPTER 20

Budweiser Showdown

Okay here we were, searching for a record deal. The last big show we did as a group was in November of '86. We did a show at the Regal Theatre. It had just opened up, and we were one of the local acts that opened up for a big-name act. We were on the show with Whodine and Four by Four. The show was a success. We did great! After a couple of months had passed, someone from the Regal Theatre recommended us to be in the Budweiser Showdown Fest.

This was a contest that included at least ten thousand other acts throughout the United States. The winner of this contest would get a chance to perform in L.A. before a group of stars and recording companies. They also would get a chance at a recording contract with C.B.S. Records.

So we sent three original tunes in. For the Midwest area, there were three winners selected. It was us, a group called Triple Three, and another group our management company managed. All three of us had to compete in another contest at the Taste Entertainment Center. The first- and second-place winners' tapes would be sent to the finals. So here we were getting ready to do a showcase contest. Oh boy! Since the band and we were on bad terms, Carl said Pierce would get a band together for us—a professional band with guys who knew what they were doing—guys who could read music and learn a show in one day! Okay, believe this if you want to.

We began practicing in Tyrone's apartment. We had no other choice. We were actually stepping and dancing in the man's apartment. We practiced, and we practiced. We learned three original songs for this contest. All the time we were rehearsing, we were preparing ourselves. This was our break. We figured that since we were asked to be in the contest, it was meant for us to win. Every day we would practice. We kept asking Carl when we were going to rehearse with the band. He said soon! As you might have noticed, when we were with our old band, we practiced every day with them, especially for a big show like this contest. We always had our act together, but Carl put this in our heads. Carl said, "We are a good group. As long as we got our act together, it will be a piece of cake when we get with the band." So we said hey, we'll do it his way.

So here we were again, time was closing in on us. We'd been practicing for a whole month and still we hadn't rehearsed with a band. We kept calling Carl and asking, "Hey, what's up with the band?" Carl would say, "Please don't worry." Well, we got to the day before the show and still we hadn't rehearsed with a band. This wasn't us at all! We began to panic! As usual, everybody started getting attitudes and blaming each other. We blamed Carl, Carl blamed Pierce, and Pierce blamed someone in the band. Then it all got blamed on Superior Movement! So we practiced one time with this band, one time before a big show like this. Everybody was tense.

We couldn't believe this was happening to us. We would never do a show with just one rehearsal, and especially if we had never done these songs with the band. But Carl began to sound like Smitty. "This will show the professionalism in you. You guys been together this long, you don't need a lot of practice. You're professionals!" Well the jokes were on us. Just think, after fourteen years of sacrificing, rehearsing, and struggling, here it was—our biggest break! If we won this part of the contest, we would go to the finals in L.A. Everyone knew that we were getting ready to make it.

CHAPTER 21

The Night of the Budweiser Showdown

Well, here it was again. Showtime everyone! We just knew that we were going win this contest. It was announced on the radio, and posters were spread throughout the city of Chicago. We knew we were the number-one act in Chicago and that this was our contest. No one could tell us that we weren't going to win. It was in our blood. We told everyone to show up, although we didn't care if they didn't, because we knew we had it in the bag!

A couple of our old band members were there. They wanted to see who we had playing behind us. They heard about us and the new band we were supposed to have. A couple of friends and relatives also came to support us. But that was it. We didn't have as many followers there as we thought we would. The other groups brought a lot of people with them. It was a full house at the Taste Entertainment Center.

We were the only group from the West Side. The other two groups were from the south side of Chicago. We had brand new uniforms for this contest. We just knew we had this contest all wrapped up. First of all, the lady from the Regal Theatre recommended us to get in this contest. Second, we knew one of the judges. Third, a guy from WBMX was dating one of our cousins. WBMX helped to sponsor the whole event! So everything was in our favor! Since we were the most popular group of the three bands that were competing, the people at WBMX suggested that we go on last. But the other groups did not agree with this. They said we should pull tags to see who went on first, second, or last. So we had to pull tags. We pulled the first tags, so we had to go on first. We didn't mind, because the sooner the better. We just knew we had this thing wrapped up. There was no way we were going to lose this contest.

Once again, it was showtime. The band began to play. We were very tense, but there was nothing we could do. We came out, and the crowd began cheering. We began singing, and wouldn't you know it! Two of the microphones weren't working. But we played it off. Then they finally got the sound together. We didn't feel the force that we usually had on stage, but we had to continue. We were on our last song and bam! All hell broke out! We were supposed to do a skit at the end of our last song. When we got to that part, everyone was very, very tense. The band didn't catch it, and neither did we. We were looking at each other on stage out the corner of our eyes. I was waiting on Billy, Billy waited on David, David waited on Tyrone, Tyrone waited on the band, and the band waited on us. Some of the audience knew and some didn't. Our showmanship covered it up. We finally got out of this spot and took our bow. The audience clapped on, and off stage we went. Overall, it still was a good performance.

After we were off the stage, we went into the dressing room. People were coming backstage to congratulate us. Dr. Lawrence Gregory Jones, who was a D.J. and one of the judges of the contest, came backstage to congratulate us on a good performance. But we knew in our minds that we had messed up on the last part. But as I said before, it still wasn't a bad performance.

Next, the other band that L.P.M. managed came on. They were too much like the Times. The Times were a very well-known, established group already. Our manager had copied the Times' style a lot. They had too many people in their band. It was more like an army. Overall they were okay, but we knew we had them beat!

Then the third act came out. I must admit, they were good. But I didn't think they were better than us. This group got to their last song, and the girl in this band hit a high note. The crowd began to roar. They finished the song and went off the stage. They got a standing ovation. People were coming by us saying we had them beat. However, one of my friends was saying that he didn't know. He said the other group was good, but he still didn't think they were better! So here we were waiting for the final decision. We all thought we had this contest wrapped up. Although the last band got a standing ovation, we just figured they had a lot of friends there to give them moral support. When they made the announcement that we came in second, we all dropped our heads. They said we lost by eleven points. We just couldn't believe this. So we all snuck out of the club one by one, hoping no one would see us leave. All the way home Tyrone and I didn't say anything. Second place was hard for us to accept. Every contest we had won; we had come in first place.

The following week after the contest we began calling each other on the phone. Everybody was blaming each other for what had happened. We even blamed the people at WBMX. We just couldn't face the fact that we were second. Even now, we still believe that something was crooked in this contest. Even though we came in second place, we still had a shot at the final in L.A. There still was hope, because the first- and second-place winners' tapes were qualified to enter the regional finals.

We finally got over this and began preparing ourselves in case we were selected winners of the regional contest. Since they were going to select the regional winner by tapes instead of live performance, we continued to work in the studio. We recorded several more tunes. It seemed like we were getting better and better at recording. Every time we recorded a tune, it would sound as good as the one we recorded previously. We were enjoying the studio more and more.

After several calls to Texas, where the headquarters of the entire contest was, we learned that we were not selected as winners of the regional. They said that a group from Kentucky had won. Another let down, but hey, it wasn't going to stop us. We knew that we had some good material, and all it takes is the right person to hear it. Our material was really getting good to us. We knew that if we kept going and kept recording, something was bound to happen. After all, too many years had been put into this group for nothing big to happen.

CHAPTER 22

Second Time Around for a Record Deal

Believe it or not, here we were again! You're probably saying to yourself, what the heck is going on? Believe it! We were saying this too.

Carl called a meeting. He said that we needed a record out and fast. So here was the game plan. We needed to put a record out ourselves. This was really a challenge for us. We never thought that we would ever have to put a record out ourselves, but if it had to be done, we had to do it!

Everybody's minds were concentrating on putting a record out. Then all of a sudden, Jenita Contrell stepped in! I bet you're saying to yourself, who in the heck is Jenita Contrell? She is the only person in Superior Movement's history who Superior Movement hated. We never thought we would hate anyone, but after what she did to us, I have no respect for her. I doubt if anyone else in the group has any respect for her either. Let me explain why.

CHAPTER 23

The Jenita Contrell Story
(Deal with Motown)

Jenita Contrell was a young lady who met the group when we had "Wide Shout" out. She was working for one of the hottest radio stations in Chicago. WGCI was the number-one station back then. At one of the outside concerts, Jenita introduced herself to Tyrone. Tyrone said after the concert he and I went over to Jenita's house and met her whole family. Maybe we did, but I swear I can't recall.

Now here five years had passed and all of a sudden Jenita dropped back on the scene. Tyrone had no contact whatsoever with her and then out of the clear blue sky, she called him. He didn't even know how she got his phone number. Jenita claims that she found his phone number in the telephone book. She said she'd been trying to catch up with him for five years. She also said that there were only three Tyrone Powells listed in the phone book, and she just knew one of them had to be him.

It was really strange the way it happened. Tyrone asked me one day if I knew a girl named Jenita. I told him no. He said she called him about 2:00 in the morning trying to explain who she was, and he decided to invite her to our next concert. He told me and the rest of the group to look out for her. He said she had long braids and was healthy. This tells us a lot, right? Well anyway, we kind of kept our eyes open. We figured that since she used to work for a radio station, she would kind of stand out from the rest of the crowd, but as it turned out, we were wrong again. Tyrone spotted her, though! I bet you know he regretted he ever ran into her. This is where our nightmare began.

CHICAGO DEFENDER - Thursday, August 10, 1989   25

Superior Movement performs on the Sound Express stage

by Earl Calloway

Superior Movement, a Chicago based vocal group that began in 1974 at Farragut High School will be featured as one of the local groups along with Tri III Band, with Stephanie Mills and Miles Jaye Sunday, Aug. 13 when the Miller High Life Sound Express returns to Washington Park, 5531 Martin Luther King, Jr. Dr.

What a joy it is to see groups who embarked upon their career during their youth, become a success! I remember the determinaton Billy Avery, Tyrone Powell, Stanley Ratliff and David Williams had when they first started performing as a group as a result of participating in talent shows at Farragut. They were members of the Boys Chorus and eventually became popular as a quartet. They really paid their dues, too. On several occasions they went to secure their fee for singing and was told there was no money. While performing once at a night club, they had to literally duck and hide from bullets that were pouring from a gun of a trigger happy drunk who had become enraged. There were harrassing experiences they suffered, however, they preservered and today they are one of the nation's most significant groups.

In 1981, Superior Movement was approached to records their first single "For You", written by the late Van McCoy. Three other singles ensured them a niche in the recording industry which was taken from their debut LP, "Key To Your Heart" released on Chicago International Music label, distributed by Epic/Portrait/Associated Labels.

The 80s found Superior Movement more involved and using their own creative inventiveness. Two

Superior Movement

years ago, the vocalists teamed with Pierre "Jovan" Downing and began exercising their own musical imagination to achieve effects that is startling and unique. In 1988 Gergory Spears was added to the group.

Jenita and Tyrone finally got re-acquainted. They began going out together. Jenita began to tell Tyrone all about herself. She told him that she worked for the telephone company and was about to get a new job at a radio station called WBMX. She said that when she used to work at WGCI, she and the station owner of WBMX were very close friends. His name is Carey Mayo. Jenita stated that

Carey Mayo was the godfather of her daughter. She also said that Carey and Harold Busby (the new president of Motown) were also very close friends. So hey, I'm sure you know what was going on in our minds. Record deal!

Anyway, Jenita said Carey could get us a deal with Motown if we wanted him to. But there was an inside catch. Tyrone made a deal with Jenita. He promised to marry this chick if she could pull this off. If she could get Superior Movement a record deal with Motown, Tyrone would be her beautiful husband. Tyrone *married*? No way! He was supposed to be the playboy of the group. But he was ready to bend if Jenita got us to Motown. Besides this, Jenita wasn't the prettiest thing around either! She was not just healthy, she was over healthy. The broad weighed at least two hundred pounds, and those braids! It looked like she let her little daughter put them in for her. You know how little girls put braids in dolls' hair? Jenita's hair was an exact duplicate. Now I don't like talking about anyone, especially if she was going with one of my buddies, but after what she did, I can't help it.

The only reason Tyrone even spent time with her was because he thought she really cared about him and that she was going to get us this record deal. Jenita was so convincing. She'd played her role to the T. She could have gotten an Oscar for what she put Superior Movement through.

Tyrone began telling the group and the management that Jenita could get us a deal. She said she would give Carey Mayo a tape of our music, and if he liked what he heard, he would get his friend Harold to hear the group. Jenita called Tyrone one night and said that she was over Carey's house and that he had listened to the tape. She said he loved our music. She put Carey on the phone to talk to Tyrone. Tyrone said that Carey told him that our music had a unique sound. He said that it was different, and we sounded young and fresh. Tyrone said that Carey said he would get his friend Harold to sign us up. He said that Harold owed him a favor, so it wouldn't be a problem.

After hearing all this wonderful news, we began rejoicing. The group hadn't been in such high spirits in a long time. We just knew that all our prayers were answered. We finally were going to make it big! As a matter of fact, this is what inspired me to write this book. My spirit was so high.

We began telling all our friends and relatives. We didn't say too much because we know from the past that we could be let down in one day. Even our manager Carl was more enthused. We began having meetings regularly on how we were going to deal with this situation. Carl said he would have to hear from Carey Mayo himself before he could believe anything. So two weeks went by, and no call from Carey. However, Jenita called Carl and told him that Carey had sent the tape that he had to his friend at Motown in California. Carl said that if Motown liked what we sent, then most likely they would ask for more material. About two or three weeks later, Jenita called Carl and told him that Carey told her to tell him to send more material to Motown. We knew this might happen, so we went back into the studio to make sure our tape was put together as professionally as possible.

All of the time, Carl was still puzzled, because everything he heard was coming to him third-hand. He was following along because the whole group really believed everything was true. Carl was even more convinced when Jenita gave him the correct address of Motown. She told him to send the package to the president of the company, Harold Busby. Now think for a second. How would she know the address to Motown and who its president was if no one told her or if she hadn't done any research? We asked ourselves, why a person would do any research on a record company for us, especially if she wasn't getting anything out of the deal. No, I take that back. She would have gotten Tyrone's hand in marriage if she pulled it through.

So now the panicking and the long waiting began. At this point, Motown was supposed to have two demo tapes and a promotional package of ours at their company. The first tape had about three or four tunes on it. Carey was supposed to have sent this tape. The second tape had about five tunes on it. This tape Carl sent himself to Motown. So we knew for sure at least the tape that Carl sent was there. We waited a whole month, but still no one called Carl from Motown. So Carl called a meeting one night. Something was terribly wrong.

We began analyzing the situation again. Everyone was looking directly at Tyrone. After all, he brought Jenita into the picture. It had been about a month and a half since this whole ordeal started. By now we should have heard something directly from Motown. So here we were, Superior Movement and Carl discussing the situation. We kept asking Tyrone what was up. He said he didn't know. He said that Jenita said that Carey would call Carl and explain to him what was going on. Another week went by and still no call from Carey. Tyrone began putting pressure on Jenita, and finally she said that Friday Carey would call Carl. That night we were all waiting for Carey to call, but again no Carey. So Tyrone picked up the phone and called Jenita. He began screaming and hollering, "What the hell is going on!" She began crying. "You don't believe me?" Jenita said. She said she would call Carey right then on her three-way phone so that she could clear the matter up. Carl turned on the intercom to the phone so that we could hear Carey, Jenita, and him talk. Carl asked Carey what was going on. Why hadn't anyone contacted him? Carey said he didn't know. He sounded unsure. Carey said that he would call Harold and get back with Carl. Well, at least now Carl was in contact with Carey. Before it was third-hand, and now it was second-hand. So things were getting a little clearer now—at least that's what we thought. Another week went by, and nothing happened. Tyrone began to come down hard on Jenita because we were coming down hard on him. She said that in a matter of days, we should hear something. So believe it or not, it happened. Jenita called Carl at his job, screaming her head off. She sounded so excited. "Carl, Carl, did you get a telegram? I've got one from Motown. Ooh, ooh, I'm so happy." Carl said he had to calm her down. She said she would give it to Tyrone, and he would give it to Carl that night. That night an emergency meeting was called. Everybody was excited. We couldn't believe that finally our dream was coming true. As the group was riding over to Carl's house for the meeting, we drank about two bottles of Champagne. We were very, very happy. We knew that one day all our suffering and sacrifices would pay off.

So here we were at Carl house. Carl began to talk. "Fellows, there is a slight problem. If you look up in the left-hand corner of this telegram, you will notice that this telegram wasn't sent from California. The return address is from Riverdale, Illinois." This was the town where Jenita lived. Everybody in the room got quiet. "I knew it was too good to be true!" Billy said, "Maybe it's a scam!" "She might be a con artist." This is what I said. I said this because I've been conned a couple of times in my life, and it's not easy to con me. But everyone at the house didn't listen to me. They thought I was just saying something out of my head. Again the finger was pointed at Tyrone. After all, Tyrone brought her to the group. He spent a lot of time with her. He even gave her a key to his apartment!

At first Tyrone was hanging tight with Jenita because she was really going to get us the record deal. Then he fell in love with her because she convinced him that she liked him for who he was and not for being an entertainer. Jenita bought Tyrone clothes and jewelry. She took him out to eat and to concerts. She was doing a lot for Tyrone that no other person would do for him. Therefore, he kind of fell in love with her. Tyrone even introduced Jenita to his family. That's how deep it was. He even called out to California to let his brother and sisters know that we'd be out there soon. Tyrone had convinced me and the other guys in the group that Jenita was a true person and that everything was going to work out like she said it would.

Now here we were at Carl's house discussing the telegram. If Jenita had sent it, why would she go through all of this? Didn't she know what we'd been through? So we told Tyrone to get her on the phone right then! Tyrone called her five times that night. Finally she answered the phone. Tyrone was very, very angry. If you knew Tyrone, you wouldn't want to be around him when he's angry. He is the one person in the group who when he gets mad, he gets mad! He's like a mad maniac! You do not mess over his group! That's what I liked about him.

Anyway, when Jenita answered the phone, Tyrone asked her what the hell was going on. She replied in a sweet and innocent voice, "You don't love me anymore?" Tyrone said, "Yeah, I love you." Everyone in the house stared in dismay. We couldn't believe Tyrone got soft hearted. It wasn't that he was soft hearted, though. Everybody has a heart. I don't care who you are. Tyrone had just lost his mind for a second. That's all it was.

Well, after Tyrone came to his senses, he began screaming and yelling at Jenita. "Don't you know what the hell you're putting me through? Why is your address on this telegram?" She couldn't explain. She said she'd call Carey to find out what was going on. So she called Carey on her three-way hook up. So picture this. The group was over at Carl's house listening to the intercom attached to the phone. Carey, Jenita, and Carl were on the phone. Jenita asked Carey to explain why her address was on the telegram. He couldn't explain. Carl eventually called out to Motown in California to verify the telegram that same night. They didn't even know who in the heck Superior Movement was. Carl asked to speak to Harold Busby, but he wasn't in. Then Carl asked Harold's secretary if she knew anything about the telegram that was sent. She said no. She said that if Harold was going to do anything with Superior Movement, she would know about it. She also said that there was a meeting later on and that after the meeting, she'd get back with him. She never called back.

Carl then called Western Union to see if they could tell him where the telegram was sent from, but they couldn't give him any information. After this Jenita called back and said that Carey said that everything would be cleared up the next day. So this is what we went by. We didn't want to believe that this whole thing was a fraud, so we again took Jenita's word that everything would be cleared up the next day. All the way home we were feeling puzzled. We just couldn't believe this was happening to us. All these years and no one had put us through the ringer like Jenita did. We all kept saying to each other, "Maybe everything will be all right." After all, the only people who knew about the telegram were us, our families, and our closest friends.

News about Superior Movement travels faster than the press in our neighborhood. This is because a lot of people believe in us, and a lot of people know what we've been through. They knew our goals and what we were aiming for. So they were just as excited as we were. When we got back to our homes, we didn't tell anyone what was going on. I mean nobody! It would hurt so bad to tell anyone. We didn't even tell our wives or girlfriends. All we could do was just wait until the next day and see what would happen. I couldn't even sleep that night. I doubt if anyone else in the group could either. All that night I prayed. I asked the Lord to please let everything work out tomorrow. If we ever needed him, we needed him now. So many people believed in us, and it would hurt so bad to let them down.

Tyrone and I worked at the same place. We told everyone that we might be getting a deal, so they knew it was in the making. I saw Tyrone the next day at work, he looked like me—depressed and broken down. We couldn't wait to get off work so we could find out what was going on. When we got off, we went straight to my house and stood by the phone. David and Billy were doing the same thing. We called each other for about an hour. Finally, about 5:30 that evening, Carl called and said he got another telegram. This one had the right address on it. It was even typed on yellow paper. The first one was on blue and white paper. Everyone's spirits were high again. Sound the bells! Superior Movement would be signing with Motown!

CHAPTER 24

Motown Sends a Telegram

Hey! Hey! Hey! Superior Movement was finally getting their big break! The news spread all over Chicago without the press. After nineteen years of singing, we were actually getting our big break.

The telegram stated that Motown had received our materials and that they were pleased with our sound. It also said that Harold Busby would be working specifically with us on this project and that the contract would be in the mail within weeks. "Once again, we welcome Superior Movement to Motown."

The next day Tyrone, Jenita, my girlfriend Antoinette, Tyrone's sister, Tonya, and I celebrated at my house. We bought drinks and toasted to our success. We were having ourselves a ball. Jenita kept saying, "See, Tyrone, you all didn't believe me. I told you! Believe me." Then Jenita started to talk about how she and Tyrone were going to get married and enjoy success together. Tyrone and I started to talk about what kind of business we were going to invest in. We couldn't believe that we were finally getting our chance in life. A couple of days later the whole group got together and celebrated. Then after a week of celebrating, we had another meeting over at Carl's house.

Carl said to us, "Fellows, something must be wrong. I still haven't heard anything directly from Motown!" It had been two or three months, and we hadn't heard directly from Motown. Tyrone then called Jenita from Carl' house, "Jenita! What's going on?" Jenita said she didn't know. She said she'd call Carey. She called Carey that night and said that the reason the contract hadn't come yet was because Harold was going to bring it himself to Chicago. He would definitely be there by Thursday. So again, we had to wait. When that Thursday came, we all were waiting by our phones to see if anyone had contacted Carl. Carl took off work that day because he didn't want to miss any phone calls. About 5:00 p.m., I called Carl to see if anyone called, and he said no. Then I called Tyrone.

"Tyrone, have you heard anything?"

"No, man, nothing yet," he replied.

All of our telephones were ringing every half an hour. We kept on calling each other hoping and praying that somebody had heard something.

Here it was 11:00 p.m. that Thursday night, and Jenita finally called Tyrone and told him that Harold Busby's plane had been delayed because of the rain. She said he was supposed to check in tomorrow at 12:00 for sure. It did rain kind of heavy that day, so she had a legitimate excuse. So again, believe it or not, we had to wait. Carl stayed off work Friday. He said maybe someone would call.

Here it was Friday, October 31, 1988. I called Carl from my job at about 3:00 that day. "Carl, did anyone call?" I asked.

"No, Stan, I don't know what's going on,"

Carl replied. When I got off work that day, Billy, David, and Carl all had left messages on my answering machine. They wanted to know if I had heard anything. I called everybody back and told them that I haven't heard a thing. Everybody was asking about Tyrone. Where was Tyrone? I didn't know. No one heard from Tyrone all that day. I saw him at work, but we didn't say much to each other. He was kind of mad because everybody was blaming him. Nevertheless, Tyrone finally called about 11:00 that night. He said that Harold had checked in at one of the hotels downtown. He also stated that Harold and Carey were together. Tyrone got all this information from you know who—Jenita! Jenita said Harold and Carey were just hanging out on the town and that tomorrow at 12:00 they would meet with Carl at the radio station Carey owned. Okay! Cool! Now we were getting somewhere. Jenita also said that sometime tomorrow morning Harold would call Carl to confirm the meeting.

So Saturday morning came, and again we waited by the telephone. I didn't want to call Carl before 9:00 a.m. because I knew no one would call that early. Ten o'clock came, and the phone began ringing like hot cakes! Everybody in the group was calling.

"Stan, have you heard anything?"

I would reply, "No, have you?"

This went on until about 7:00 that night. Now where in the heck were Tyrone and Jenita? Tyrone had spent the night over Jenita's house.

Tyrone finally called about 8:00 and said that Harold and Carey were at the convention that day. We couldn't believe this was going on. What about the contracts? How long does it take to drop contracts off? This didn't make sense at all. Tyrone said that he and Jenita were going to go to the hotel where Harold was staying. He said they were going to wait until they returned. Several members in the group had called down to the hotel to see if a Harold Busby had ever checked in. Sure enough, he had a reservation, but he'd never checked in. Then we asked Jenita, and she said he didn't check into that hotel. She said he checked in at a hotel that was closer to the convention.

Everybody was getting sick of this. We just couldn't believe this was happening. All we could do was just wait. Wait, wait, and wait. All day Sunday we waited. After about 11:00 that night, we were like chickens with our heads cut off. We didn't know what the heck was happening. We just couldn't believe that a person would put us four guys through this. We didn't do anything wrong to deserve this, unless Tyrone did something in the past to her, and she wanted to get revenge. I just couldn't see it. Tyrone said he didn't do anything to her that would have hurt her. Then we had three managers who also had to suffer through this. Carl had contacted people all over the United States, people like booking agencies and promotional companies. As soon as the deal was finalized, we would have been on our way. People were ready to help us.

On Monday, Carl finally caught up with Carey Mayo at WBMX. He said that he didn't know what Carl was talking about. He said that he was very, very sorry. The person who Carl talked to over the phone was somebody imposing as Carey Mayo. Jenita had set the whole thing up. The real Carey Mayo said he knew Jenita but he hadn't seen or heard from her within a year.

Can you believe this! This was the dirtiest trick anyone had ever played on Superior Movement. For three months the girl had us and our management company in the palm of her hand. We could have put a record out ourselves had Jenita not come into the picture. We had never been so hurt as a group before. Our spirits went all the way down. We didn't rehearse for about two months. No one had the enthusiasm, although we did keep in touch off and on. It was very hard to face our friends and relatives. We told them and they told their friends, and now we found out it was all a hoax. We never did find out who the guy posing as Carey was.

Even after all of this, Jenita had the nerve to keep calling Tyrone. If you ask me, I think the girl was really sick. The nerve of this chick!

CHAPTER 25

After the Storm

I called this next chapter after the storm, because the Jenita incident is considered a storm. It was hell, and now we had to regroup ourselves. It was very, very hard to get back into the swing of things. It was like taking the last breath out of somebody. But then again, it made us kind of stronger. We didn't do any shows for a while. What we did was to go back into the studio and try to put something even better than what we had already. This went on for months. Then we sent more tapes out to record companies, yet we still had no deal.

Rehearsal began to get boring again. David brought up the idea of getting a fifth member. First he said Calvin. We all said no in unison. Then Billy brought up a guy named Greg. We asked him who Greg was. He said that Greg used to sing with various groups around town. He said he seemed to be serious about his music. At first the rest of the group said no, and then we said we'd try him out.

Greg came to rehearsal for about a month, but we never did let him know if he was an official member of Superior Movement. Then, out of the clear blue sky, guess who called? That's right—Calvin Ford called up everybody in the group. He said that he deserved to have another chance. He damn near begged us to put him back in the group. Calvin even went to some of our closest friends to try and get them to persuade us to let him back in the group.

Finally, like fools, we gave in. We let Calvin back in. As for Greg, we kind of ignored him for a while. We told him that there were no rehearsals. Now Billy really didn't want Calvin back in the group, but he did it for us. At first things looked as if they were going just fine. We started to rehearse like old times. We cracked jokes on each other and got things done. Then all of a sudden, Calvin went back to his old ways. We should have known, but we were stupid. Billy was 100 percent right. He said Calvin wouldn't work out. Every time we had rehearsal, Calvin was always the one not to show up. He did this about three or four times, and finally we said no way. We didn't have time to put up with this kind of behavior. We weren't about to let him hold us down.

CHAPTER 26

Greg Becomes an Official Member

So back to Greg we went. Greg said he knew something was up. He couldn't believe that Superior Movement didn't rehearse for three weeks. However, he put this behind him, and so did we. We began rehearsing harder than ever. As it turned out, Greg added a new dimension to the group. He could lead sing, dance, and he knew how to rap! Right away we told Greg he was an official member of Superior Movement. Rehearsals were greater than ever. Everyone was pleased with how rehearsals were going.

Then we said we had to get a band. We began looking. This guy named Cliff came by my house three or four times. He said that he heard we were looking for a band. I told him that the band we were looking for had to have updated equipment. They also had to be serious about their music, because we were not getting any younger. If we were going to come out one more time, we were going to do it right, everything from singing to band, to uniform and to management. We got together and started to do shows off and on. Greg was working out. We all felt that he was one of us. We met his family and began rehearsing over at his house. We didn't do many shows, but at least we all had the same goal: making it big in the music business.

CHAPTER 27

Things Begin to Slow Down

Things began to slow down. We weren't doing many shows. We weren't rehearsing like we used to. Everybody seemed to be losing interest. Most of us began using drugs off and on. Tyrone and I would drink rum and coke every day. Then we graduated to marijuana; then eventually started snorting cocaine. We then started to free-base, but I didn't like the feeling. So when we bought cocaine, I would snort it and Tyrone would free base it. Eventually we got together with David and Calvin. As time went on, we started to do drugs with other friends in the neighborhood. This began to separate us even more. Billy didn't know what was going on. He had a gut feeling, but I don't think he knew exactly what was going on. Billy never used drugs as far as I know.

As time went on, I began hanging out with a friend of mine who I used to work with. His name was Donnie. I hadn't seen Donnie in two years. I was riding in the school's van, taking some of the students home, and I ran into Donnie. We exchanged phone numbers, and he ended up over my house the following weekend. He told me that it was his birthday and that he had no one to celebrate it with. I told him to come on up, and he did. He brought along with him some marijuana, beer, and cocaine. As we were indulging in our activity of getting high, my fiancée, Antoinette, entered the room complaining about the car note that needed to be paid. Then she left the room.

Donnie asked me if I needed to borrow some money. Of course I said yes. I used to always borrow $10 to $20 from him when he used to work at the school, but this time I needed a lot. I told him to lend me $500 and I would pay him back something every time that I got paid. He then asked me if that was all I needed. I told him since he asked it like that, I could use $1000. I didn't know if he really had the money until we went to his car and counted out ten $100 bills. You should have seen the smile on my face. I told him, "I promise I will pay you back." He then told me to come and take a ride with him. To my surprise, we went to a bar. Donnie told me to sit at the bar while he went in the back with the owner and did a drug transaction. After this, he took me home.

The next day I was hanging out with him again. The same thing happened at another club. He took me to one of his many girlfriends' houses and showed me a suitcase full of money. I was amazed at how he had so much money. He even owned a limousine! We used to ride around in the city drinking and riding. I never asked him for anymore money because I was enjoying just being his friend. Donnie also used to play cards a lot. Every weekend I would go with him to one of his friends' houses and there would be a card game going on. I used to sit on the couch all night long while he played cards. I couldn't believe that people would play cards in their home with thousands of dollars stacked on the table.

The people that would be playing were sheriffs, politicians, and ordinary people. Antoinette and I would always get into arguments and fights because she said that I was changing. I didn't see it that way. All I knew is that I was hanging out with my buddy, and she didn't like it. Donnie used to pay for Antoinette and me when we went out. All the time I didn't realize that one day I would have to pay for hanging out with Donnie. All of my life I had never hung out with anyone selling drugs. I had always been associated with people doing positive things. But things began to change when I was hanging out with Donnie. He was a good-hearted person, but when he realized the police were setting him up, he put me into the picture.

This is what happened. I was on my way home after dropping off some of my students. I used to drive the school's van and take some of the students home. I was allowed to take the van home because I had to pick the students up in the morning as well. As I was riding down Washington Boulevard, I noticed Donnie's van parked. I knew that he was over at his friend's house because we were just over there the week before. I remembered that Donnie told me to stop by his house when I got off work. I was supposed to pick some money up from him because he was going to pay for some tickets to the O'Jays concert.

Well, since his van was parked, I figured that I would stop and pick the money up now. I rang the bell, and someone buzzed me in. I went to the third floor and knocked. Someone opened the door partway and told Donnie that I was at the door. Donnie came to the door and said, "Let's go." On the way down the stairs, he gave me the key to his van and told me to drive. I said to myself, *Maybe he will tell me where we are going when we get in the van.* Donnie never came to the van.

I thought that he was getting in on the passenger side of the van, but instead he got into a car that was parked in front of the building that we had just come out of. When I got into the driver's seat of the van, I looked out of the window and noticed that Donnie was arguing with a lady who was in the driver's seat of the car. I had never seen him so angry. After about five minutes or so, Donnie got out of the car, got into the van ,and asked me to give her a bag. It was a Walgreen's plastic bag. I couldn't see what was inside of it, but I had a notion that it was drugs, jewelry, or money. I really didn't care. I asked Donnie why he wouldn't give it to her. He replied, "Just give it to her!" I thought that this was one of his girlfriends and he just didn't want to be bothered with her.

So I took the bag and rationalized. I didn't know what was in this bag. I didn't look inside of it, and I was just going to give her the bag and leave. It did not work out the way I thought it would. As I approached the driver's side of the car, the lady gave me a hand motion to come to the other side of the car. I thought that she wanted me to tell Donnie something, so I got into the car. When I got in the car, she began to count off $100 bills. "One hundred, two hundred, three hundred, four hundred." I stopped her and told her that I was going to get Donnie because I didn't know what was going on.

As I reached for the door handle of the car, about fifteen policemen were there with their guns drawn. They pulled me out of the car and had me lay face down on the ground. They had Donnie on the ground across the street. Then they took us to the police station in Bellwood. At the station, the policemen were telling me that I would be released soon. Donnie told me that he had written a statement that I had nothing to do with what had just happened. As the night passed away, we were taken downtown to the police station on 12th State. They told us that they would be transferring us to the county jail in the morning. The county jail! That's serious! I had never been arrested in my life, and now I was headed to the county jail. I couldn't believe it!

We were transferred to the county jail and had to have a bond hearing. When we got into the courtroom, I noticed that the judge was black and a female. I said to myself, *This sister knows how the system is messed up. She knows how crooked the policemen can be. When she reads the testimony that Donnie wrote on my behalf, I will surely be set free.* I was wrong again. As we approached the bench, the judge made a decision and posted both Donnie's and my bond each at $100,000.

Cook County Jail—26th & California

Now let me remind you that my job only paid me $8,000 a year. Where on earth was I going to get $10,000? Whatever amount the judge said, the defendant has to pay 10 percent of it. In my case, I had to come up with $10,000. That's a lot of money! I began to lose hope, because I knew that I didn't know anybody who had that kind of money. So immediately I began to pray. "Lord, Lord, Lord! You know what happened, and you know that I didn't have anything to do with this case. You are God, and you know all things. I know that I shouldn't have been hanging out with Donnie, and if you can just help me out this time, I will start going back to church." Well, the Lord heard my prayers.

Some may have called it luck, but I knew that deep down in my heart it was the Lord answering my prayer. Donnie had gotten out on bond the next day. Antoinette had found out, and she began calling his house every hour on the hour. Donnie couldn't get any sleep because she was calling him telling him, "You got Stanley into this mess, now you get him out of it!" Donnie eventually gave up $6,000, and my mother had gotten $4,000 off of her visa card. I knew that only God could have pulled this off.

When I got out on bail, at first I tried to avoid going to church. I thought that everyone would laugh at me because I got into a little trouble and now I was running to the Lord. God began sending me signs that I needed to be closer to him. I had several of my cousins who had grown up in the church come by my house and tell me how God would work it out for me. I remember going to the Post Office to pick up my unemployment check. A lady handed me a tract that said Jesus loves me. At this point I remembered my vow to the Lord. The only church that came to mind was Lawndale Community Church. My friend and former football coach was the pastor. His name is Wayne Gordon, but everyone still calls him Coach. Now I hadn't seen Coach in about fifteen years, but I was led to go and talk to him about my situation. I had also lost my job at Hillside Academy because of this. Well, when I finally made it to Coach's office, I began to tell him that I was in a little trouble, but when I went to court everything would come out as to how I got involved and they would then release me. Coach prayed for me and then invited me to come to church on Sunday.

When I came to church, I saw three other guys from our 1976 football team. They were also going through some heavy trials in their lives. One guy was hooked on drugs, another was going through a marriage problem, and another had an alcohol issue. Back in the late 70s we were all part of FCA Bible study group. We used to go over to Coach's house, and he would teach us the Bible and take us to different churches on Sundays. Unfortunately, we didn't take those Bible studies seriously. I think that we were doing them more for Coach's sake than our own. Now here we were fifteen years later, and we needed God more than ever. Coach suggested that we start meeting on Wednesday mornings before everyone went to work to have a Bible study. I was always the first one there. All of a sudden the Bible began to be real to me. It was as if everything that I was reading was talking about me. I remember reading about David and some of his trials, and all I could see was myself.

Franklin Park

For the first time in my life I was beginning to enjoy reading the Bible. I even began having a Bible study in my house with Antoinette and my cousin Sonya. We all started to go to church every Sunday. Even though we started to go to church every Sunday, we still weren't ready to change our lives around. We would wholeheartedly get together after church and buy alcohol and drugs. It seemed to be the normal thing to do. Every time I went to court, I would return to the Bible study group and tell them that the case was continued. It would be the same routine for about eight months. I would go to court and they would call me and Donnie up to the judge's bench.

Donnie's lawyer would say a few words to the judge, and my lawyer wouldn't say anything. The judge would always be drinking coffee and reading a newspaper during these procedures. Then he would say, "Let's continue this until the next month." I couldn't believe that this case went on like it did. My life was on hold. I began to get depressed, wondering how I got myself into this. It wasn't supposed to be this way. I was wondering why everybody who was involved with this case couldn't come out together in the courtroom at the same time and say, "Hey, Stanley wasn't involved with this." Why couldn't the judge and the state's attorney read the testimony that Donnie had written and just let me go? After my hearing, I realized why it couldn't happen like that. I saw first-hand how corrupt our judicial system really was. This is how my hearing went.

For eight months they would always call Donnie and me up together. This particular time, they called Donnie up by himself. They did not call me up with him as they would normally do. Donnie accepted a plea bargain and received ten years. However, they let him go home for thirty days, and he would have to turn himself in after the thirty days.

Then they called me up to the bench by myself. They asked me if I wanted a bench hearing or a jury trail. I told them to give me a jury trial, because I figured if a group of civilized people heard how I got involved with this case that they would surely let me go. However, it did not work out this way. My lawyer brought Tyrone in as a character witness on my behalf. Tyrone knew me very well, and he had also worked at Hillside Academy with me. He then invited Antoinette as another character witness.

After this I took the stand. I began to cry and tell how I really didn't know what was going on that day. Then my lawyer called the undercover officer that set everything up with Donnie the day of the incident. My lawyer asked her if she had ever seen me prior to the day of the incident. She replied, "No." He then asked her that when I got into the car if there any conversation about drugs or money. She said no. My lawyer then asked her if I reached for the money as she was counting it. She said no. Finally my lawyer tried to present the statement that Donnie had written about me not having anything to do with what had happened that day. The state's attorney objected, and then a side bar was called. The judge, state's attorney, and my lawyer went into a small conference about the statement my lawyer was trying to present to the jury. The judge decided that the statement was hearsay and that it could not be used in the case. So the jury never knew that Donnie wrote a statement that I was innocent. I didn't know that this kind of stuff happens in the court. I thought that everything would be presented and then someone would decide if someone else is guilty or not. I was thinking that all the undercover agent had to do was tell the truth, that she didn't know me, that she had never seen me or spoken to me, and that I had nothing to do with her or Donnie that day.

But such is the case of many young black boys who don't have the right kind of representation when they go to court. They get railroaded into a corrupted judicial system and then are assigned a number for the rest of their life. I knew that they were out to get me from the beginning, because the state's attorney's opening statement to the jury, which was 99 percent white and 1 percent black, was: "Ladies and gentlemen of the jury, that young man sitting over there is Stanley Ratliff. He is responsible for bringing drugs from Colombia to Chicago. He delivered the bag of cocaine to the undercover agent, and therefore you must find him guilty." I said to myself, *Surely they will never believe him. First of all, this man doesn't even know me. If he knew me, he would have known that I have never left this country for anything. As a matter of fact, I haven't been out of Chicago in years. So how can he say that I'm responsible for bringing drugs from Columbia to Chicago! Doesn't he have to prove this?*

I began crying because I wanted the jury to see my tears and maybe they would at least look into the case a little deeper. Perhaps someone on the jury would say, "Maybe he is innocent." When the state's attorney gave his closing argument, he reiterated to the jury that I gave the undercover agent the bag and that they must find me guilty. After deliberating for about four hours, the jury came back with the verdict of guilty. I was shocked, blown away! I couldn't believe it! The sheriff handcuffed me and began taking me out of the court room. Antoinette and Tyrone began crying.

While I was in the back, my lawyer came to visit me. He said that he went to one of the jurors and asked them why they came to the conclusion that I was guilty. The juror replied that I lied on the jury stand. He said that I stated that a week prior to the incident Donnie and I were watching a college football game with some friends. He said that I lied because it was basketball season at that time. Let me remind you that this incident happened eight months to a year before we actually had the hearing. I was nervous; I was scared while on that jury stand. Who cared about what I was watching? All I knew was that we were watching sports. I thought that it was a college football game. Hey, it could have been a video tape! God knows I wasn't trying to lie or make anything up. I'll admit to this day that I shouldn't been hanging out with Donnie, but I never had anything to do with the deal he had between the undercover agent and him.

To me it seems like someone on the jury had to be prejudiced or they wanted everyone else on the jury to think that they were wise. But in actuality, they weren't wise at all, because if they were in my place, they probably would have said the same thing. When you are on a jury stand for the first time in your life, who wouldn't be scared? I had no reason to lie. The only reason I stopped that day was to pick up some money from Donnie to get some O'Jays' tickets. Nothing else!

Well, need I say anything else? I was off to prison, but the group continued to sing off and on. My dream was shattered. All the goals I had of making it big were over. I thought to myself that I'd let myself down, my family down, my friends down, and more important, I'd let my group down. I felt so embarrassed and so humiliated. All my life all I wanted to do was to be successful in music. In grade school I played the saxophone from third grade through eighth grade. When I went to high school, the school that I was attending didn't have a saxophone for me. So I made a decision to join the male chorus. Then we started Superior Movement. I went to college and majored in music so that I would be an asset to the group. It was not supposed to end this way, but it did. The group finally broke up.

As of now, Tyrone lives in California. He works at the airport. David still works downtown and attends a church in Maywood, Illinois. Calvin passed away in 2005. I couldn't attend the funeral because I was out of town that week. Smitty, our manager, also died. Greg sings at a church located on the west side of Chicago. Billy has been a mailman for years and is on the praise team along with me at the Lawndale Community Church. I am the director of Hope House (a Christian recovery home), and I am also the Minster of Music at the Lawndale Community Church. Coach Wayne Gordon is the pastor of this church. We really tried to make this thing work. A lot of hard work, sweat, and tears were put into Superior Movement. It was a dream, a goal, but never a reality.